*I consider Mark Drake to be the finest
alive today! I guarantee this book will*
-Larry Silverman- Pastor, Author

*You do not know me. I'm not anyone important. But none of that
mattered to God. I received your book from my pastor and it changed
my life.* **–Donna-**

*Ordered your book. Read it! Loved it! Now, almost every page is
underlined, starred, double starred, with comments, dog-eared pages,
bracketed sections, and more comments.* **–KB T-**

*Mark Drake's books have changed my life. After being in a cult for 14
years, the freedom I have found in Christ is more than I can say.* **–CP-**

*The New Covenant Grace that Mark teaches is so easy to understand,
practical, applicable and life changing. He sows his life into the next
generation and has translated his grace-base books into more than a
dozen languages, at his own cost, and then gives them all away.*
–Sam Surendran, Lead Pastor, Excel Point Church, Penang, Malaysia

*Mark Drake takes those 'way-over-your-head' spiritual concepts and sets
them in a tone of clarity and freedom. His work, his writings, and his
teachings have been groundbreaking, refreshing, and transforming.*
-Steve Roberts, author, teacher, poet, Penang, Malaysia

*I honestly do not know of anyone who has captured the true essence of
the meaning of grace, as Mark Drake has.*
-Micah Smith- Pastor, Author, International Missions Director

*Mark has written great books, but he IS a book; his life has been an open
book that has read by people around the world. He, too, has been well-
worn; a little dog-eared and pretty beaten up in his "earthly tent"
through all the miles he's put on it as he's traveled the world. But he still
has more books in him and more miles to go before he's done spreading
the truth about the miracle of Christ in us, the hope of glory.*
–Brad Brisson, Pastor

Running On Empty

*How Weakness and Failure Can
Unleash Transforming Grace*

MARK DRAKE

Why god must run us out of our own strength
...for our eternal good!

I hold to the statement of deep theological thought from the most high and holy reverend theologian, Dr. Seuss.

> # Sometimes the questions are complicated and the answers are simple.
> ### -Dr. Seuss

Do you have questions about how to live in the power and freedom of true grace? Have you read verses that seem to contradict the message of grace? Have you read or heard people teach things that are confusing about how grace works?

Apparent contradictions and confusing questions can have simple answers and Mark can help you find them. Go ahead, ask Mark and get answers by email.

Your answers become part of the world-wide digital library Mark's team is building to help people everywhere get the answers they need.

askmark@markdrake.org

HELP! TYPOS- Each time I write a book, I do my best to have the manuscript proofread by many friends. But no matter how well we do, we seem to always miss some. When you find them, please send me an email so we can correct them in the next printing. I, and future readers, thank you!

Mark and Linda Drake

I owe much of my understanding of these truths to Craig Dahlberg. As a true friend, he taught me how to face painful truths about myself, that integrity is far more important than success, and, much to the relief of my wife, Linda, he taught me how to truly love my wife.

Craig and Jackie Dahlberg

Life is easy when things are going well. But failure changes everything. The way Craig and Jackie have lived their lives openly and honestly, demonstrates what it means to hang on to the Faithful God through painful failures, broken dreams, and crushing betrayals. I owe them both so much for being our loyal, lifelong friends.

-Mark Drake- St. Louis, MO, USA

If this book helps you, please send me a note and tell me about it at markdrake.org...
...AND TELL YOUR FRIENDS!

As an independent author, our ministry depends completely on friends telling other friends about our books. Please share your thoughts with your friends on Facebook, Instagram, etc.

Want to help people in the world's poorest countries get free grace materials? Join our team at **markdrake.org**. We have one goal- Equip Leaders Worldwide To Spread New Covenant Grace!

Join our support team of monthly partners, help us equip leaders around the world, and leave a legacy of your own!

Running On Empty

*How Weakness and Failure Can
Unleash the Transforming Grace*

Chapter One

He Can, He Does...
And Sometimes
He Doesn't

I have been on this journey in Christ for more than forty-five years, most of those years in full time ministry, and I believe in miracles. I believe in completely inexplicable acts of God.

I believe in a God who miraculously intervenes on behalf of His children. I believe in a God who delights in doing for us the miraculous things we cannot possibly do for ourselves.

I believe in all the *"suddenlies"* in the Bible; the places where people were helpless and utterly hopeless, unless God intervened...and suddenly...He did! And I believe He still does.

My wife and I have lived over four decades depending on God's miraculous intervention and we have seen Him prove Himself completely faithful!

> **I believe in all the "suddenlies" in the Bible**

I pray for the sick to be healed, I pray for prosperity to come, I pray for marriages to be healed, I pray for hearts to be miraculously changed and I ask for nations to be shaken by the goodness of God and the revelation of Jesus Christ as Lord of all. I spend most of my life traveling around the world in some pretty dangerous places and I trust the Father for divine

1

protection. I believe His angels take care of me and coordinate His plan for my life.

I do not believe my life is subject to the whim of earthly powers, either seen or unseen. I believe that this adventure of learning how to cooperate with Christ, who is living in and through me, can be accomplished only by the miraculous power of the Holy Spirit.

Integrity Demands That I Also Admit-

Based on the testimony of God's Word, and the matching evidence of real life, I must also admit;

> -*Many don't get their physical healing in this life.*
> -*Many suffer the pressure of unmet financial needs.*
> -*Hearts sometimes get hard and divorces happen.*
> -*Good parents sometimes have children who make really bad choices, no matter how much the parents pray.*
> -*Bad parents sometimes have children who make really good choices even though the parents don't pray.*
> -*In this world, "bad things" happen to "good people."*

I believe God *does* intervene with miracles and delivers us out of many adverse circumstances. And I believe that He often times *does not* deliver us out, but empowers us from within to go through trials, tribulations and suffering. I believe He has eternal reasons for both of these conflicting life experiences.

And I believe that if those of us who believe in miracles are not careful, we may sometimes unintentionally struggle against His purposes; to our own great frustration. Why? Because, as human beings, bound by time and space, we have an extremely limited understanding of how He works all circumstances together to fulfill His eternally good plan for us. (Rom. 8:28)

And in all of this, I rest in the amazing peace of knowing that God does indeed make all things work together for my eternal good. (Rom. 8:28)   I often don't understand it, but I do believe it.

Both Realities Are True-

I believe that both of these inescapable facts of life are true. God does miraculous things in the lives of those who trust Him. And many times, He who has the miraculous power *to do*, chooses *not to do*. I cannot escape the fact that He who has the power to deliver me *out of a problem* frequently wants to empower me to *go through it.*

The Bible is filled with undeniable evidence of this great paradox. Our God does show up with miraculous intervention. And sometimes He has a completely different plan for us. Our God does sometimes demonstrate His power by miraculously, instantaneously delivering us from our troubles. And sometimes, He empowers us to suffer through our troubles so we will learn to never trust our own understanding, never trust our own wisdom, never trust our own strength; and never put **our faith in our ability to have faith**!

After all these years of study and life experience, I am fully convinced that God wants to teach us how to live the journey of this Christian life expecting His miraculous care. And just as importantly, He wants us to learn to live in unwavering peace and abounding joy when our miracle doesn't come *when, where or how* we want.

> **Our God does show up with miraculous interventions.**
>
> **And sometimes He has a completely different, and always better, plan for us.**

It is very important, for those of us who believe that our God is still in the *"miracle working business,"* to understand that all miracles in this present, fallen world are only temporary. They are important, very important. But they are only temporary. They serve a very important purpose in God's plan for mankind; but they are only temporary.

Was Lazarus All That Thrilled?

Lazarus was raised from the dead. This is not just a nice, comforting fable; it really happened. But after his miraculous resurrection, he had to live on in this fallen world a little longer and then die all over again. That miracle was important, but it was only temporary. It is possible that the only one who wasn't all that thrilled about this resurrection was...Lazarus.

> MIRACLES ARE IMPORTANT BUT THEY ARE ONLY TEMPORARY. TRUSTING HIM IS ETERNAL!

Jesus really did feed over 5000 people by a miracle of multiplying fish and bread. But it was only temporary. They got hungry again, just a few hours later, and they had to feed themselves. That amazing miracle served God's purpose of helping prove that Jesus was the Christ, the promised Messiah.

But for those people who ate the miracle food, it was only temporary. And their fickle faith shows that miracles may not always produce the results we hope they will. It is very tempting to think that if we can just empty out a hospital then all will believe. History proves this is just not the case. The Pharisees saw the miracles and claimed they were from the devil. The "multitudes" saw the miracles, ate the bread, and helped crucify Him.

> **Miracles don't always produce the results we hope they will.**

Philip was literally, miraculously *"teleported"* from the river where he baptized the man from Ethiopia and he suddenly appeared in a city many miles away. (Acts 8:27-40) I travel nearly 150,000 air miles every year and I would love to have that *"spiritual"* gift! That would be awesome. It would save me thousands of hours, hundreds of thousands of dollars and a frequently sore backside. But it's never happened.

It really did happen to Philip; but only once. And if Luke hadn't written it down, I am not sure anyone would have known about it. But the next trip Philip made, he had to do it the old fashioned way, just like the rest of us. It was an amazing miracle, but it was only temporary.

A Dangerous, Unscriptural Trap-

These miracles, and many others recorded in the scripture, really happened; but they didn't *always* happen. And it is very tempting, and dangerous, to fall into the trap of thinking that if we just have enough faith, God will always over-ride the natural laws in this fallen world and miraculously fix every problem and solve every dilemma. But that is not what the biblical record tells us.

> Miracles happened in the Bible. But not always. And we lack integrity if we pretend they did.

One day, when Christ returns for the *"restoration of all things,"* (Acts 3:21) paradise lost will become paradise fully restored. And then the *"supernatural laws of nature"* will be the norm and work miraculously in our everyday life. But that Day has not come yet, no matter how much faith we have. (Acts 3:21)

5

It is also very tempting, and dangerous, to fall into the trap of thinking that if people could just see a bonafide miracle, then they will truly believe. However, if we keep on reading the biblical account of these stories, we find that many of those same people who saw those amazing miracles never came to truth faith; and just a short time later they joined the crowd that crucified the Lord.

Their failure to believe doesn't negate the true reason God did these miracles. And it doesn't negate the fact that some of those people came to faith in Christ after Pentecost. But this, and many other Bible stories, should help us keep the miraculous in a healthy scriptural perspective.

As young hippies, converted in the late 1960s, many of us prayed for the Beatles, or the Stones, or the Doors, or Janis Joplin (or fill in your personal favorite) to somehow come to faith in Christ. We just knew that if that happened then everyone would believe. But, it didn't happen and they wouldn't have all believed even if it did happen.

> **Oh, if only the Beatles would have come to faith in Christ!**

God has very real and important reasons why He invades our time/space world and does amazing, mind-blowing miracles. And He has very real and important reasons why He doesn't.

Is There A More Important Purpose?

God does sometimes answer prayer with amazing miracles. And sometimes He doesn't. Unless we are willing to read the entire biblical narrative and actually give serious thought to the context of what we read, this seemingly contradictory truth can cause great confusion in the lives of sincere believers. This confusion becomes a powerful tool of the enemy unless we see there is a greater, more eternal truth at work in our lives than the quick, temporary solving of all our problems.

I am convinced of this because I am learning that God has some over-riding principles, some undeniable truths that are far more important for eternity than any temporary miracle. Here are a few of them.

God must run us out of our own strength.

He must exhaust our human effort.

He must frustrate our human understanding.

He must break our desire for formulas and lead us into a new and living way of fellowship.

And He must lead us into dying to our own best efforts, so we can experience His resurrection life being lived in and through us.

He must run us out of our own understanding. He must run us out of our own ability. He must run us out of our own feeble efforts if we are to produce a life that would be pleasing to Him. Then, and only then, can we fall to the ground and die, like a grain of wheat, and begin to experience the resurrection life of **Christ in us, the hope of glory!** (Col. 1:27)

> "Unless a grain of wheat falls into the earth and dies, it remains alone; but if it dies, it bears much fruit." (John 12:24-25) NASB

Our well-intended human efforts actually get in the way of His eternal process working within us. So He must fully exhaust us with hard, adverse, and frequently

7

confusing circumstances before we can ever experience the most amazing miracle, the most awesome reality, the most satisfying experience in all eternity: *the reality of Christ living His divine life in us and through us!* If the Son *"learned obedience through the things which He suffered"* (Heb. 5:8), then what does that say about us?

Some May Stop Reading Right Here-

I know I may have already lost some readers. I realize that I may be misunderstood. I understand that some may feel I am somehow teaching unbelief. I hope you are not one of those because this journey into New Covenant faith requires a living, growing trust in a faithful heavenly Father. And there is a very real battle involved with this kind of life.

I hope you can hear my heart as we struggle together to find a place of biblical honesty. Find a place of scriptural reality. And a doorway into the truly abundant life He wants for us! And I hope you will continue on with me as we journey into the place where there is unwavering peace and abounding joy for any who are willing to die to themselves and their own understanding. And that is what we have been promised- a *"peace that passes all understanding."* But for us to get a peace that passes all human understanding, we have to allow God to put us in circumstances we cannot possibly understand!

I am convinced that we can trust the Father to use every trial, every pain, every confusing situation to raise us to newness of life; *Christ's life, living in us and through us!*

> **To get a peace that passes all human understanding, we have to allow God to put us in circumstances we cannot possibly understand!**

And please remember as we go- I do truly believe in miracles!

I have come to love this adaption of a statement made by Dr. James Richards.

> *The journey of the heart is such a paradox.*
> *To hunger for wholeness...but to accept where I am;*
> *To want change...but stay in a place of rest;*
> *To know something is missing...*
> *and be happy that I will find it on the way;*
> *To hunger for it all now...*
> *but love the fact that I will spend eternity discovering it.*

Join Me On This Journey Of The Heart-

I urge you to join me in this amazing adventure of learning why **God must run us out of our own strength**. Only through this painful process can we fully experience "death," so that His resurrection life can be fully lived *in us* and *through us*!

I understand this journey can sometimes be a confusing one, filled with seeming contradictions. I know it has been for me.

But I think we are going to find that most of the contradictions come because we haven't actually _read the whole story._

Chapter Two

I Have To Read The Whole Story

There is a very real danger in reading short portions of the Bible and drawing conclusions. The danger is, more often than not, we will be completely wrong. It is absolutely critical to read the whole story, to see the full context, to read the word of God accurately, and interpret its truth with integrity.

As I travel the world, investing my time in equipping young leaders with the tools to read the Word accurately and interpret it with integrity, I teach them to focus on three simple concepts.

1) **Consider Context-** Always read several verses before and after the passage you are examining. Understand who wrote it, why they wrote it, and who they were writing to.

2) **Comprehend Culture-** Literature written two thousand years ago is influenced by the culture in which it was written, at the time it was written. Fortunately for us, most cultural information is often just a computer click away.

3) **Compare Similar Scriptures-** The letters of the New Testament were not intended to be complete explanations of truths. They were short reminders written to people who had already been taught. In

order to get a full understanding, we have to compare all the verses that relate to each specific subject.

As we proceed, let's keep these three things in mind-

1) Consider Context
2) Comprehend Culture
3) Compare Similar Scriptures

As with all ancient writings in "*dead languages*," the study of these can go as deep as we choose to go. But the good news is God deliberately inspired the biblical writers to communicate divine truth in ways anyone can understand with a little bit of effort and a dose of common sense.

Even though over 95% of the people in the first century could not read, Peter tells us that the Holy Spirit gives us all we need for life and godliness. We may not understand every prophet, judge or king. But we can learn enough to grow in God's grace and mature in righteous, Christ-like behavior.

> "*His divine power has given us <u>everything we need for life and godliness</u> <u>through our knowledge of Him</u> who called us by his own glory and goodness.*" (2 Peter 1:3-4)

Most false teaching or bad doctrine comes when people pick and choose small portions of scripture instead of reading the whole story. "*Reading the whole story*" is just another way of saying we must consider the "*before and after*" context of any passage we read. If we don't read the whole story, we will make assumptions about God, His nature, His character, His behavior and what He will or will not do; and we will be wrong. The result will be fear, confusion, and even anger towards Him when He doesn't act the way we thought He should.

Most Basic, Important Rule- CONSIDER CONTEXT!

Let's take Acts 12 as an example. If we start reading at verse 3, we see an amazing story of miraculous deliverance for Peter.

> When Herod saw how much this pleased the Jewish leaders, he arrested Peter during the Passover celebration and imprisoned him, placing him under the guard of four squads of four soldiers each. Herod's intention was to bring Peter out for public trial after the Passover. But while Peter was in prison, the church prayed very earnestly for him. The night before Peter was to be placed on trial, he was asleep, chained between two soldiers, with others standing guard at the prison gate. Suddenly, there was a bright light in the cell, and an angel of the Lord stood before Peter." (Acts 12:3-10 NLT)

You probably know the rest of the story. God miraculously intervenes, the angel delivers Peter from prison, Herod is not able to kill him, the church rejoices and Peter has many more years of fruitful ministry.

If this is all we read, it would be natural to conclude that any time we get into trouble, we can claim this promise of deliverance and believe that God will, and must, miraculously deliver us. If we don't read the whole story, then it would be logical to conclude that this is an orthodox, trustworthy belief because, as some teach, *"If God did this for Peter, then He must do it for us, every time. God is no respecter of persons!"*

But what if we don't get delivered from our trouble? What if we continue to suffer through our trial? What if, instead of things getting better when we pray, things actually get worse? What are we going to believe now that our conclusion about God and what He will do for us does not hold true?

> **What if we don't get delivered from our trouble?**

Faulty Conclusions Come From Not Reading the Whole Story-

Based on only the portion of scripture we read in Acts 12:3-10, we could easily come to some depressing conclusions about God and about ourselves, if God does not deliver us.

We could easily come to believe, as some teach, that God was somehow unfair or unfaithful if He doesn't deliver us the way He delivered Peter...then He would be to blame.

Or, as some teach, God would be a liar because if He didn't do for us what He did for Peter, then His promise wouldn't be true...so He would be to blame.

Of course, few of us would have the honesty to say that we actually thought God was to blame for not helping us the way we expected. Or that God was somehow a *"liar"* for not delivering us as He delivered others. We may feel it, but few would ever say it out loud. Until the confusions becomes too much.

At one time in my life, I did say it, out loud, I screamed it. I don't

> **Is God to blame?**
> **Am I to blame?**
> **Is the devil to blame?**

recommend it unless you're ready for truth. But for me, it was the best thing I could have done. It moved me toward His truth.

14

But if we are trusting God for our miracle, and it doesn't come, we may feel the pressure to come up with some kind of an explanation. So we may come to a different set of conclusions to account for why we didn't get our miracle.

We could choose to believe, as some teach, that we just didn't have enough faith. So even though He wanted to, God couldn't deliver us because of our lack of faith...so we are to blame.

Or, as some teach, there is some *"hidden sin"* in our lives so God must withhold His help...so we are to blame.

Or, as some teach, we didn't pray enough...so we are to blame.

Or, as some teach, we didn't have enough intercessors praying with us, doing *"spiritual warfare"* for us...so we are to blame.

The conclusions we draw from those times when God does not deliver us *when, where or how* we want are extremely important...and very dangerous! Dangerous, because if we believe any of the above conclusions we will be wrong, seriously wrong. All of these faulty conclusions come from human logic, not from God's Word. But they will seem biblical because we took them from what we read in Acts 12. But they are dangerously wrong because we didn't *read the whole story*.

We didn't read the whole story!

The story actually begins, not in verse 3, but in verse 1-

> *"About that time King Herod Agrippa began to persecute some believers in the church. **He had the apostle James (John's brother) killed with a sword.**"* (Acts 12:1-2)

15

Then we see the portion of the story we read earlier, starting in verse 3, *"When Herod saw how much this pleased the Jewish leaders, he arrested Peter..."*

We Begin To See the Whole Story-

Herod began persecuting the church and, because James was one of the main leaders, Herod had him killed. Then he had Peter arrested with every intention of killing him, too. But God miraculously delivered Peter before Herod had the chance.

Wait a minute. Now I am really confused.

James was a great apostle, one of the twelve. He was arrested and killed. His ministry was "*cut short.*"

Peter was a great apostle, one of the twelve, and he was also arrested. But he got a miraculous deliverance and continued on in ministry for several more years with a great testimony to tell. And if it were today, he would have a great testimony **to sell**.

So what conclusions do we draw now that we know the whole story? Now that we know that Peter got his miracle but James did not, what are we supposed to believe?

How often have we heard that *"no weapon formed against us will prosper?"* (Is. 54:17) It certainly seems that a real "*weapon prospered*" against James. Was God unfaithful to James? Did God lie to James about His promises of deliverance? Didn't James have enough faith? Did he not pray enough? Were there not enough people praying for James? Was the church praying for Peter but

> Was God unfaithful to James? Did the devil win by cutting short a vital ministry?

16

not praying for James? Was God punishing James because of some *"hidden sin"* in his life and Peter didn't have any sin? Was James to blame for his death? Did he die prematurely? Did the devil win by killing off a great man of God too soon?

These are very real questions that our adversary uses to steal our confidence with God and torment us with fear, shame, and condemnation. These are questions that have caused painful torment in the lives of many sincere believers. So much torment in fact, that some have given up out of confusion, hopelessness, or bitterness; feeling that they have either failed God or God has failed them.

But what if all these questions are actually unbiblical diversions from the real question? What if the real question in times of painful crisis is not about getting free from our troubles, but about learning how to trust that God has a plan for our lives in the midst of the trouble? And what if the biblical answer is actually simple? What if the right conclusion is uncomplicated and plain?

It may seem to be contradictory that God would deliver Peter while He let James die in the same situation. But on my journey into a faith that produces rest and peace-filled trust in God, I have come to believe that the right answer to this seeming contradiction is this- the same God who had the power to deliver Peter also had the power to deliver James.

But God had a different plan for James, just as He has a plan for all of us. And here's why I rest in this kind of faith.

> **The same God who had the power to deliver Peter also had the power to deliver James. So why didn't He?**

17

God Had Very Different Plans For James And Peter-

Jesus had already prophesied to Peter that he would live to an old age. After the resurrection, Jesus told Peter,

> *"The truth is, when you were young, you were able to do as you liked and go wherever you wanted to. **But when you are old**, you will stretch out your hands, and others will direct you and take you where you don't want to go." Jesus said this to let him know what **kind of death** he would die to glorify God."* (John 21:18-19 NLT)

History tells us that Peter did live to be an old man and near the end of his life he was arrested by Rome, held in prison, *"taken where he didn't want to go,"* and put to death as a martyr; just like Jesus said.

The simple truth is this- Acts 12 just wasn't Peter's time to die. God was not finished with him yet. Herod couldn't carry out his plan for Peter

> **Acts 12 just wasn't Peter's time to die.**

because God had a different plan. If we believe the words of Jesus then we know it just wasn't time for Peter to die.

And let's be honest; if we believe our goal is eternal life with the Father, and that the eternal is far more important than the temporal, then we have to ask ourselves, who actually got the better deal? James or Peter?

Who Got The Better Deal?

Clearly, the only *"deal"* that truly matters is the fulfillment of God's will in our lives. However, Paul understood that we live in a human body and the issue of death does matter. But as believers, we should view death completely different than the world views

18

death. Paul's perspective sheds important light on how the early believers looked at life and death of their physical body.

> *"...while we are at home in the body we are absent from the Lord, for we walk by faith, not by sight, and we are of good courage, I say, and **prefer rather to be absent from the body and to be at home with the Lord.**"*
>
> (2 Cor 5:6-8 NLT)

Paul makes his view about death very clear- *"I prefer death so that I may be at home with the Lord."* Paul fully enjoyed the reality of Christ living in him, in his mortal body (Rom. 8:11) and fulfilling the earthly calling which the Lord had entrusted to him. But he lived with the belief that his eternal life in the coming Kingdom of God was the goal he set his sights upon.

> *"Therefore if you have been raised up with Christ, keep **seeking the things above**, where Christ is, seated at the right hand of God. **Set your mind on the things above**, not on the things that are on earth."* (Col 3:1-2)

Paul was not looking to escape this present world because he was fully aware of the mission God had called him to fulfill. But he was fully prepared to go to the next when his time was finished.

> *"For to me, living is for Christ, and **dying is even better.** Yet if I live, that means fruitful service for Christ. I really don't know which is better. I'm torn between two desires: Sometimes I want to live, and sometimes I long to go and be with Christ. That would be far better for me, but **it is better for you that I live.**"* (Phil 1:21-24 NLT)

These words have had a tremendous impact on the way I look at my life and my death. Now that I am nearing 70 years old, I am

very aware that most of my natural life is over. Rather than regretting things I *"should have or could have done,"* I am being filled with joy for what is to come. Generations of believers have endured untold suffering and death because they believed Paul's words, *"Living is for Christ and dying is even better."*
Listen again to Paul's words, again.

> -Living is good but dying is even better.
> -Sometimes I long to go and be with Christ.
> -But it's better for you if I stay.
> -So I guess I'll stay a little longer.

These are not the words of a man suffering from depression or self-pity. These are the faith-filled words of one who had his eyes and heart set on the Kingdom that is to come! And he was completely content to let the Lord unfold His plan *when, where and how* He wanted.

This is the same man who spoke to his fellow Jews about King David and said *"For David, **after he had served the purpose of God in his own generation,** fell asleep..."* (Acts 13:36)

> *"...after he had served the purpose of God*
> *in his own generation..."*

What amazing confidence! What awesome trust! David had his share of failures, sins, troubles, and trials. Sometimes he saw God's mighty deliverance and sometimes he suffered through great difficulties.

However, he served the purpose of God in his own time, and then he went to be with the One in whom he trusted. The only way to understand David's life is to read the *whole story*.

Peter had his share of failures, sins, troubles, and trials. Sometimes he saw God's mighty deliverance and sometimes he suffered through great difficulties. He didn't always do the right thing or make the right choice. Sometimes he reaped difficult circumstances but he always saw God turn everything out for his eternal good.

He could endure all these situations because he learned the secret letting Him live in and through him. Peter learned that each time God ran him out of his own strength or understanding, he grew in God's transforming grace.

But why don't we let him tell his own story.

Chapter Three

Peter, Stop Making Promises

Something was wrong. Something was very wrong. I could not have heard Him correctly. This can't be right. I just swore my allegiance to Him. I promised I would never forsake Him, but He rebuked me and told me to stop making promises about remaining faithful. How can those promises be wrong? What does He expect me to say after what He just accused me of? What is going on here? (John 13:21-38)

For three and a half years we had followed Him. We had given up our friends and our families, our jobs and our futures, all because we believed He was the One. People said we were crazy to believe this guy. But we were so sure He was the One, we couldn't help but believe and follow. Now He says He's leaving us and we can't come with Him. This can't be right. This is not the way this was supposed to go. It can't all end this way.

He was supposed to be the King. We were supposed to be leaders in His new Kingdom. He was supposed to crush Rome and put Israel back in charge. We were supposed to have favored seats in His new government. We have pinned all our hopes on Him, and now He says it's over? This is crazy!

We've done everything He has asked us to do. When the Pharisees threatened to kill us all, we stayed.

> We pinned all our hopes on Him, and now He says He's leaving us?!?!

Even when all the crowds turned away because of that bizarre talk about "eating His flesh and drinking His blood," we stayed. We still don't understand what He was talking about back then, but we stayed. And now He says it over, He's leaving us; and He has the audacity to say, "This is for your own good"! (John 16:7) He can't be serious.

You Will All Forsake Me, And It's OK-

He just told us that, before the night was over, we would all forsake Him. He just looked us all right in the eye and said we would all fall away. And He acted as if this was somehow going to be OK, somehow it would all work out for good.

I told Him that He was wrong. We were the ones who had given up everything to follow Him. Doesn't He appreciate the commitment we have shown? The promises we've made? And how can He act like this will all be OK?

I guess I could understand about these other guys. They have all been confused, they have all struggled to believe, and they have all waffled at one time or another. And if it's really going to get as bad as He says, then I guess I can understand why He would question their determination. But not me! (Matt. 26:33)

> *"I can understand how these guys might fall away, but not me. I promise!!"*

And I told Him that. I told Him that I had seen the weakness in these other guys and I could see how they might give up out of fear. But not me! I would never betray Him. I told Him I would never go back to my old way of life, no matter what it cost me.

And I think, after all that's happened, He should know me well enough by now to know that I mean what I say.

I Know You Better
Than You Know Yourself-

After all of my promises, He said that He did know me. In fact, He said He knew me better than I knew myself. And then, He rebuked me right in front of the others guys. I have to tell you, it was embarrassing to hear Him talk like that in front of my friends. I mean, if He really questioned my commitment, at least He could have taken me aside to tell me. He has certainly done that before.

But, instead, He started talking about the devil and how satan had demanded permission to test me, to "sift me like wheat", I think He said.

I told Him He was wrong. I told Him that nothing could make me deny Him. I told Him I was willing to die for Him. But then He got this strange look in His eye and told me to just stop talking, to stop making promises.

This was so confusing, so frustrating. I didn't understand what He wanted from me. I told Him I wasn't going to leave Him, no matter what. I promised Him I would die before I would betray Him. I told Him that it didn't matter what the other guys did, He could count on me.

> "We've been threatened before. It didn't move me then and it wouldn't move me now."

And I honestly thought that's what He would want me to say. We're supposed to be faithful, aren't we?

25

I Don't Understand This-

But I just couldn't understand what was happening. That whole night had been weird. It seemed like everything I said was wrong.

The first thing He did when He walked in the room was to look around at each us and start washing our feet. That didn't seem right. He was the leader, He shouldn't be doing that. I know we were all standing there with dirty feet but there should have been a servant to do that kind of dirty work, not Him.

So when He knelt in front of me with that basin and towel, I told Him this wasn't right. But He looked up at me and said, "You can't understand this now, but later on you will."

Frankly, I was getting a little tired of hearing that. I mean, after all this time and all we've been through together, you'd think He would give us a little more credit and just tell us what was going on. To tell you the truth, I got the feeling that He sometimes really enjoyed seeing us so confused!

But it seemed really important to Him that we all get washed, so I said, "Lord, don't just wash my feet, wash all of me!" Apparently, that wasn't the right response either. I just got another rebuke. I just don't know what He wants from me.

> I just don't know what He wants from me.

The dinner just got stranger the longer it dragged on. We finally sat down to eat and Jesus suddenly starts talking about betrayal and He didn't seem to be bothered by it at all. Everything felt so surreal. After all we had been through together; and now He's talking about disloyalty and betrayal like it's just all going to be OK.

Then, right in the middle of dinner, Judas got up and left. Jesus had leaned over and said something to him about "go on and do what you're going to do," and then he just got up and left. None of us understood what was going on. I leaned over to ask John if he knew what was going on, but he didn't understand it either. (John 13:21-30)

I Am Leaving You-

That's when He started this talk about leaving. It didn't seem to make any sense. We had just entered Jerusalem with the largest, most enthusiastic crowds we've ever had and now He's talking about leaving us.

> Right the middle of the biggest crowds yet, and now He's leaving?!?!

I couldn't stay quiet any longer, so I asked, "Lord, where are you going?" And that's when it suddenly got very personal...and very painful.

He turned and looked at me; and it almost seemed as if He felt sorry for me. "Where I am going now, you cannot follow. But you will follow Me later."

After everything that had happened that night, I felt like my loyalty was being questioned, so I said the only thing I knew to say, "Lord, why can't I go with You now? I promise You, I am ready to die for you!"

That's when He started saying the most bizarre thing I had heard Him say in all our time together. After all He had taught us about faith, miracles and overcoming the devil, this certainly didn't fit in with what I thought was the victorious life He was offering us in return for following Him.

I Have Given Satan Permission-

He had just finished talking about the Kingdom He was going to bring, and how we would sit with Him, eat and drink at His table, and how we would rule in this new Kingdom. And then, out of the blue, He said to me;

> *"Simon, Simon, satan has asked to test and try you. He has asked to have the power to sift you like wheat. And I have given Him permission to do it." (Luke 22:31)*

My mind was reeling as I tried to understand where this was going and what it meant. Why would He be telling me this now, when we are on the verge of seeing the Kingdom fully come? And if He really loved me, why would He agree to let this happen to me, now, when we were so close? But He wasn't finished.

> *"Simon, this is going to happen and it's going to be bad. But I have already prayed for you so that when you are sifted, your faith will not be completely blotted out. And when this is over, you will turn around from the way you have been going and you will be able to strengthen your brothers with a strength that is not your own."*
> *(Luke 22:32)*

I just couldn't take it all in, it felt like my mind was about to explode. In fact, I didn't even hear much of what He said after that. All I could think was, "No, I will not let this happen. I cannot let this happen!"

> *"I did the only thing I knew to do; I promised, with all my heart and strength."*

So I did the only thing I knew to do; the only thing I thought was right. I promised, with all my heart and strength, I promised Him that I would be faithful.

28

But I Promise, And I Really Mean It-

> "Lord, I will not do this. I will not forsake You. In fact, I swear, I will not forsake You. I swear to You, I am ready to go to prison...no...I am ready die before I will forsake You!"
> (Luke 22:33)

Then, with eyes that seemed to say He understood my confusion and a voice filled with compassion, He quietly said,

> "Yes, Peter, you will indeed swear. You will swear you don't know Me. In fact, before the rooster crows tomorrow morning, you will curse and swear three times that you don't even know who I am. Peter, all your promises to Me are going to fail." (Luke 22:34)

I was dumbstruck. I couldn't say a word. I don't know if I was overcome with shame that He would think so little of my commitment to Him or just ashamed that He would accuse me of this kind of betrayal in front of my friends.

I was so shocked that I didn't even hear what He said next. "Peter, stop making promises and listen to Me". John told me much later that Jesus continued to talk, but I didn't continue to listen. And that was my biggest mistake.

Looking back now, I think maybe if I would have kept listening to the rest of what He had to say, I might have had a lot more faith for the unavoidable crisis that was to come. If I would have just listened instead of defending myself; if I would have just trusted that He knew me better than I knew myself; if I would have just believed

> "Jesus continued to talk, but I didn't continue to listen. I just kept defending myself."

that He knew what He was talking about, that He knew what was best for me...

Maybe You Don't Understand Either-

Oh well, you know the rest of my story. But perhaps, you don't really understand the rest of my story. Perhaps you don't understand that this whole episode was the very best thing that could have happened to me. It was a gift from God to me. I could never have become the man I am now if this would have happened any other way.

I can hardly believe I am saying this, but I am so very grateful for everything that happened that night. It was the hardest thing I have ever experienced. It was the most painful time of my life. And the embarrassment nearly killed me.

But it really was the best thing that could have happened to me. I really thought I meant what I was promising and I thought that promise was what He wanted from me.

But now I understand. I died that night. All my promises died. All my good intentions died. All I thought I understood about following Him; it all just died. And by the time it was all over, I discovered what this New Covenant is really all about.

Oh, He did leave us just like He said. But He came back just like He said. He came back by His Spirit in a way we could never have understood. And He has been living in me and through

> *Now I understand. I died that night. All my promises died. All my good intentions died. And that's good."*

me ever since. And I am on a journey of learning that the more I die to my own effort, the more He can live in me.

I am learning that He doesn't want promises from me. He isn't interested in my great declarations or "faith confessions." He just wants me to be completely honest and brutally truthful about my utter helplessness without Him.

And to my constant surprise, I am changing; changing into the man I have always wanted to be. And it's all because I stopped promising; I stopped trying so hard to defend myself and just received His grace; the transforming power of Him living His life in me and through me.

Me, the guy who really thought I could do all this by my own effort. But He had to run me completely out of my own strength so I could discover the secret of real life in Him! And I am a grateful man.

Oh sure, I had to get over the embarrassment of knowing my story was written down and every believer knows about the mess I made that night and the painful days that followed. But, you know what? He has turned all that for my good. And He has turned my failure into good for everyone who has read about what I did, learned from it, and chose to put their trust in Him instead of themselves, just like I learned to do.

I really hope that my pain, my embarrassment, and the lessons I learned, will be good for you, too. And if you don't get anything else from my story, learn this: Stop making promises and keep listening to what His Word and Spirit are saying.

Remember, put your confidence in the same thing I finally learned to put my confidence in- Him, living in me, doing the work I can't do.

> **Him, living in me, doing for me what I can't do.**

31

If you will let Him run you out of your own strength, burn you out completely of your own wisdom and your own understanding, no matter how painful it may be; He will put His life, His power, and His strength inside of you. And you will enjoy life, life more abundantly!

-Peter,
A servant, grateful to have died to my best effort and to be made alive in the Spirit!

Chapter Four

Keep Listening, He's Still Talking

The story you read in the previous chapter really happened just like I recorded it. Obviously, I took some literary license and worded it in a little more modern English, and I connected the facts by merging the different accounts found in the four Gospels into one complete story. When you compare the whole story as told in John 13-16, Luke 22:13-34, Mark 14:17-31 and Matthew 26:19-35, you will see that it unfolded just as I have written it.

And this story of how Peter betrayed the Lord, how he failed, how he lied, how he cursed and swore he didn't even know who Jesus was; this story of Peter's colossal failure has been told and retold, often by fiery preachers with brimstone in their voices. The point of their message is usually about the horrible thing Peter did. And it usually ends with the severe warning that *"If you deny the Lord, He will surely deny you!"*

But is this really the lesson contained in this painful story? Was *"denying the Lord"* really the issue Jesus was trying to get to inside of Peter? Or

> *"If you deny the Lord, He will surely deny you!"*
> Wait a minute-
> What about Peter?

could it be that God took Peter through an experience that every believer after him must also go through, in one form or another?

Could it be that God was most interested in running Peter out of his own strength, exhausting him from all his human promises and

33

crushing Peter's trust in his well-intended human effort so that something miraculous can happen inside of him?

If we don't listen to the entire story, if we don't keep listening to all of His words, we will miss the real reason Jesus took Peter through this seemingly devastating experience. If we don't pay close attention to what actually happened, if we trust in our own faulty human logic, we will miss the life-saving hope contained in this story.

A Dangerous Thing We Do-

Could the often repeated and dangerously wrong understanding of what actually happened that fateful night be due to a serious mistake that we Bible readers often make?

> If we don't pay close attention to what happened we will miss the life-saving hope contained in Peter's story.

I have come to believe one of the most dangerous things we do is take Bible verses out of context and pull partial thoughts of out larger portions of scripture. Then, we sincerely try to build our lives on a foundation of dangerous assumptions; without any real understanding of the truth contained in stories like this.

Could we, like Peter, be guilty of hearing only a small portion of what God's word says and then stop listening? The result? We miss the most important things God wants to say to us and we build our lives on a very shaky foundation that crumbles into fear, shame and condemnation when the storms of life blow.

One of the most important truths from the parable of the man who builds his house upon a foundation of either sand or rock is that the winds of adversity *will* blow! Jesus doesn't say *"if,"* but

34

"when." And it doesn't matter how much faith I think I have, the winds of adversity will blow and I better learn how to stand!

> *"Everyone who hears these words of Mine and does not act on them, will be like a foolish man who built his house on the sand. The rain fell, and the floods came, and the winds blew and slammed against that house; and it fell — and great was its fall."* (Matt 7:24-27)

The only way we can *"hear these words of Mine"* is to read them, and keep on reading them until we (1) understand who He was saying them to, (2) the circumstances that caused Him to say them; and (3) make sure we keep listening to all He has to say on any specific subject.

Remember-

> # Wrong expectations guarantee disappointment!

We cannot impose our human expectations upon the Sovereign God and expect Him to conform to us. If we do, or should I say, *when we do*, we will be deeply disappointed.

If we think God has promised one thing when His full Word tells us something else, then we are guaranteed disappointment. Peter was crushed, and nearly destroyed by disappointment that night because he stopped listening to all Jesus was saying.

And why did he stop listening? Because what Jesus said did not fit with what Peter thought *"the victorious Christian life"* was supposed to be. *"Falling away and denying the Lord"* did not fit in with Peter's understanding of victorious living. But Jesus knew that there can be no *"victorious living"* when our confidence is rooted in our human ability to keep our promises to God.

Only when we are run out of our own strength can we ever experience His strength, His resurrection life living in and through us! And that is the essence of true, biblical *"victorious living"!*

The Wrong Way To Read The Bible-

It seems to me that the biggest mistake I have made over the years has been reading the Bible in a way that I would never read any other piece of literature.

I love to read all types of literature. But I would never pull one sentence out of the middle of a mystery novel and believe I knew *"who done it"*. I would only make that decision after reading the entire story to truly understand what was going on. And I may have to read it several times before truly understanding.

I would never read one paragraph or even one chapter out of a history book and then claim that I understood what a nation of people did or why they did it. Instead, I would seek to understand the context, the circumstances, the feelings and mindsets of the people involved; and then draw a conclusion.

We would never walk into the middle of a conversation and assume we knew what was being discussed. OK, I confess, I have done that many times and always ended up embarrassed by the faulty assumption I made, thinking I knew what was going on. And I confess, I have done this with the Bible many times.

This is an affliction many of us suffer with. We tend to have a *"promise box"* mentality about the Bible. We pull out one verse, taken out of context, and then we want God to fit His truth into our understanding. And we don't understand, and can be deeply disappointed, when it doesn't work the way we expected.

King David wrote about the majesty of God's words in his longest recorded Psalm, Ps. 119. After writing 159 verses about the importance, power and truth of God's words, he ends with this conclusion.

> *"**The sum of Your word is truth**, and <u>every one</u> of Your righteous ordinances is everlasting."* (Ps 119:160)

*"The **sum** of Your word is truth..."* David understood that we must learn to keep listening to **all** His words if we are going to understand Him, how He loves us, and what He wants from us.

> "THE SUM OF
> YOUR WORD
> IS TRUTH"

Context, Context, Context-

When buying real estate, we are told the three most important things are *location, location and location.* This is because we understand that the value of a piece of property depends largely upon where it's located; it's *"context."* A house costs more if it's on the beach but much less if it's built next to the city garbage dump. Same house, different location, different value... different *"context."*

And so it is with the Bible. Context is critical in understanding the meaning and *"value"* of any individual passage of scripture.

Let's suppose I pull a card out of my *"promise box"* and read-

> *"God blessed them; and God said to them, 'Be fruitful and multiply'."* (Gen 1:28)

37

I would be correct in believing this is the Word of God. I might then make the assumption that God is speaking to me, telling *me* that *I* should have has many children as I possibly can.

Then in my morning devotional I open my Bible, blindly point to a verse, and I read Paul's words to the Corinthian believers in the first century.

> *"But I say to the unmarried and to widows that it is good for them if they remain even as I."* (1 Cor 7:8)

Now I have a dilemma. If God is speaking to me, what is He saying? Am I supposed to not get married...*and* have as many children as possible?

A correct reading of the Bible would show me that the context is completely different; therefore, the meaning is completely different. In one case, the earth needed to be populated. In the other, severe persecution was coming and the believers were in for a terrible time of first century tribulation that would be very hard on families.

> **When the context is completely different, the meaning is completely different.**

The Genesis command is not a law for all of today's believers to have huge families. And, Paul's statement is not a condemnation of marriage. Both passages make room for individual destinies, callings, and giftings. In fact, if we simply back up one verse in 1 Corinthians 7 to verse 7, we read,

> *"Yet I wish that all men were even as I myself am. However, **each man has his own gift** from God, <u>one in this manner, and another in that.</u>"* (1 Cor. 7:7)

By reading a little further, we see Paul's concern about the intense persecution and the horrible effects on families.

> *"Because of the present crisis, I think that it is good for you to remain as you are. 27 Are you married? Do not seek a divorce. Are you unmarried? Do not look for a wife. 28 But if you do marry, you have not sinned; and if a virgin marries, she has not sinned. But those who marry will face many troubles in this life, and I want to spare you this."*
> (1 Cor 7:26-28)

Taken in context, we see that each person has an individual gifting and destiny from God. Taken out of context we have confusion and condemnation. Taken in context...peace and fulfillment.

In Genesis we are told that in some cases God *"closed the womb."* On the other hand, some families only had one or two children, (Abraham and Sarah) while others had a dozen (Jacob). And Paul commended marriage to anyone and tells us it is to be considered as holy to the Lord. Context is critical for us to build our lives on a sure foundation of the written Word.

Heroes Of Faith?

Hebrews 11 tells us about the many

> God knew their hearts, even though their outward behavior seemed to tell a different story.

heroes of faith who accomplished great things as God used them for His unique and individual purpose. Yet, when we go back and read the actual stories of those *"heroes,"* we see that they all made terrible, often very costly mistakes. And they all struggled with doubt. By understanding the context, we see that God saw their hearts and counted them faithful, even though the facts of their outward behavior seemed to tell a different story.

39

And this fact should give us tremendous hope for our own journey. It should encourage us to know that our outward actions don't always tell the story of our hearts; good or bad.

Did Peter
Actually Fail?

And so it was with Peter. He did a terrible thing. He had an extremely painful failure. But when we read the whole story, when we listen to everything Jesus said to him, we see a very different purpose in what Peter did and the tremendous good that came out of a *"bad"* thing.

And what was the *"good"* that came out of that *"bad"* thing? Peter discovered that he must not put any confidence in his own strength or his own promises. He learned that the strength of Christ's resurrection life would live within him only when he stopped trusting his own understanding...and kept listening to all Jesus had to say. And that's the same journey we are all on!

My Strength or His Strength IN Me-

When we read the whole story, just as it is written, the Lord's words to Peter make the reasons for the events that followed very clear. The words the Lord spoke could have given Peter great peace and unshakable faith in the midst of a terrible storm; a storm that had to happen.

But Peter stopped listening to the Lord when he was offended by having his loyalty, and the strength of his promises, questioned. We must not make the same mistake. We have to hear ALL Jesus said to him. If we will, we can learn tremendous lessons that will hold us in the trials we will undoubtedly face.

> **Peter was offended by having his loyalty challenged and he stopped listening.**

This *"disaster"* was actually the best thing that could have happened to Peter. It taught him that he had to run completely out of his own strength before he could ever experience the strength of God living in him. Running to empty enabled Peter to be filled with God.

Jesus kept talking, but Peter stopped listening.

So, what did Jesus actually say?

Chapter Five

That
Terrible Night

What began as a deeply meaningful dinner with Jesus and His closest men, quickly became the most painful and embarrassing night of Peter's life. But it had only just begun.

Jesus set the frightening stage for what was to come.

> *"Peter, before this night ends, the devil will test you and sift you like wheat. All your promises will fail, your faith will be nearly blotted out, and you will curse and swear three times that you don't even know Me!"*

Peter couldn't hear anything after these devastating words. In fact, as they left the upstairs banquet hall, he, and all the other disciples, kept insisting that they would never do what Jesus had predicted. I can't even imagine how they must felt with these "insulting" words ringing in their ears.

Into The Garden-

As they left the dinner in that upstairs banquet room, they walked a few blocks down the road to the garden where Jesus began to pray. Yet, even with these words of their impending failure weighing heavily on their hearts, they couldn't stay awake for an hour to pray with Him.

After waking them up more than once, Jesus described the problem they faced as they trusted in their human effort, when He said, *"The spirit is indeed willing, but the flesh is weak."* (Matt. 26:41) They were soon to learn that this was the problem with their misunderstanding of the Old Covenant. They mistakenly believed that fulfilling their obligations to God depended on their human ability to do what, in fact, only God could do for them, in them and through them!

Little did they know that this entire, painful episode would prepare them to receive the New Covenant grace that was to come; where human effort (*the flesh is weak*) would be put to death and the power of the Spirit would come and live within them. And, oh, how they must have wished for some easier way to enter into it, but there was not. Not for them, and not for us!

> **Complete burn out, full failure of human effort is the only way to enter into New Covenant life.**

Peter Uses Human Effort, And Understanding, Again-

After a lengthy time of prayer, soldiers suddenly rush into the garden. The disciples are overwhelmed with confusion. Judas steps up and betrays Jesus with a kiss. Jesus had predicted all this just a few hours earlier. And that fact should have at least given them the strength to wait and watch; just hold on and see what would happen next.

But Peter didn't remember any of it. All he could think was that this could not be right and he had to somehow defend the Lord. So, once again, Peter acts out of his own human effort and understanding.

This must have been a horrible moment. The confusion and fear must have been extreme. But forgive me for a moment as I find some strange humor in this scene; only because I have so often seen the same kind of convoluted thinking in myself.

Peter Makes Good On His Promise-

Peter, the one who boasted how he would never forsake the Lord, now acts on his well-intended promise. He grabs a sword. Remember, Jesus told them to bring one. (Luke 22:38) Clearly, He knew the terrible mistake Peter was going to make and He made sure he would have the means to do it. I don't fully understand this. It seems bizarrely funny to me, but this is the way it happened. I doubt that I would have done any better than Peter.

Instead of attacking the armed soldiers where it might have done some good, Peter swings his sword at a servant, misses his neck and cuts off his ear. Jesus, seeing this happen, speaks to Peter, *"Put away the sword. Those who live by the sword will die by the sword."*

Remember, this is the sword Jesus told them to bring. I know how confusing this sounds. I don't think I fully understand it, either. Except that, knowing how important it is that God runs us out of our own strength, I now see that He loves us enough to set up the exact circumstances that will do the job.

Think about Jesus saying, *"Those who live by the sword will die by the sword."* That sword was the means for Peter to try to do by human effort that which only God could do by His Spirit- redeem mankind from their sins by Christ's death and guarantee our sonship by raising Him from the dead. None of this could be accomplished by the best intentions of human effort.

"Those who live by the sword will die by the sword." I do not believe this statement has anything to do with violence or war. But it's another way of telling Peter, *"Those who try to please God by promises made in human effort must be burned out of that same human effort."*

Though I cannot fully understand it, I do know that God knows exactly what He's doing and all our hope is in that absolute, though hard to understand, truth. He uses every circumstance to bring us to the end of ourselves, burning us out so completely that our lives become all about His work within us. Oh, how He wants to live *in* and *through* us!

> *"Those who try to please God by promises made in human effort must be run out of that same human effort."*

And It Gets Even More Bizarre-

If Jesus needed to be saved, He certainly didn't need Peter's human effort to do it because the next thing He says is...

> *"...do you think that I cannot appeal to My Father, and He will at once put at My disposal more than twelve legions of angels?"* (Matt 26:53-54)

And while He is saying this, He calmly bends down, picks up the ear, and sticks it back on the servant's head! In the midst of all this bizarre confusion, Jesus just picks up the ear, heals the guy...and keeps on talking! I can't imagine what the servant must have thought, or the soldiers, or the disciples. Weird.

And Jesus just keeps on talking as if this never even happened. He talks to Judas, He talks to the soldiers, and He talks to the

46

disciples. And He keeps repeating, *"All this must happen, just this way, for the Scripture to be fulfilled."*

Jesus understood that all these things had to happen, and they had to happen exactly this way, so the New Covenant could come. It had to be demonstrated, to all who were willing to see, that well-intended human effort could not bring the Kingdom of God. All sincere, but completely ineffective human effort had to be exhausted, burned out completely. It just gets in the way!

> **Well intended human effort just gets in the way of the New Covenant- Christ living in and through us.**

Now The Main Drama Begins-

Jesus is now taken by the soldiers to the High Priest, and all the disciples flee. But Peter turns and follows...at a distance.

> *"But Peter was following Him at a distance as far as the courtyard of the high priest, and entered in, and sat down with the officers to see the outcome."* (Matt 26:58)

The accusations and beatings begin. Peter can no longer endure watching this gruesome treatment of his dearest friend. So he goes out to the courtyard between the governmental buildings, where a large crowd is gathering. And then it happens, just like Jesus said. Please, don't skip over any of this.

> *Now Peter was sitting outside in the courtyard, and a servant-girl came to him and said, "You too were with Jesus the Galilean." But he denied it before them all, saying, "I do not know what you are talking about." When he had gone out to the gateway, another servant-girl saw him and said to those who were there, "This man was with*

*Jesus of Nazareth." And again he denied it with an oath, "I do not know the man." A little later the bystanders came up and said to Peter, "Surely you too are one of them; for even the way you talk gives you away." **Then he began to curse and swear,** "I do not know the man!" And <u>immediately</u> a rooster crowed.* (Matt 26:69-74)

As the scene unfolds, Jesus is being taken from the High Priest, to Herod, to Pilate. And back, again. No one wanted to take the blame for putting this man to death so they kept sending Him back and forth between these governmental buildings.

Luke gives us an amazing insight into the way in which the Sovereign Lord was orchestrating these events. Jesus is being accused, beaten, and dragged from one official to another.

And then, at the exact right moment, as He is being dragged through the courtyard, a rooster crows. Peter has cursed and swore the third time; and now, he looks up. Jesus is being taken through the courtyard at that exact moment. He turns, and through blood soaked eyes...

...He sees Peter. *And Peter sees Him*.

The Lord turned and looked at Peter. And Peter remembered the word of the Lord, how He had told him, "Before a rooster crows today, you will deny Me three times." And he went out and wept bitterly.

(Luke 22:61-62)

Words fail me. I have no way to describe how Peter must have felt, *looking up at that exact moment*, meeting the bloodied eyes of Jesus. The depth of despair Peter felt at that moment is beyond anything I have words to describe.

48

I can only imagine what Peter must have thought the moment his eyes meet Jesus' eyes and His words came flooding back.

"That's it. I've done it. Just like He said. I have utterly failed to keep my promise. I have cursed and swore I didn't even know Him. Nothing could be worse than this. And it's all over for me now. I am finished."

That's all Peter could think about.
It's all Peter could see.
Because it's all Peter remembered.

But, there is something very important Peter had forgotten.

Chapter Six

We Know Something Peter Forgot

Of course, we know something Peter forgot; something he never really heard in the first place. Something his determined self-defense could not have allowed him to believe. Not yet.

It wasn't over for him. In fact, it had only just begun. Peter had burned out completely; completely exhausted of his own strength. And it was the very best thing that could have happened to him. But he couldn't see it, couldn't have believed it, not yet.

> **It wasn't over for him. In fact, it had only just begun.**

The sad thing is that we remember something that Peter didn't remember. We are told what he did remember-

> *Peter remembered the word of the Lord*, how He told him, *"Before a rooster crows, you will deny Me three times."*
>
> (Luke 22:61)

But Peter was so overcome with grief because of his failure that he forgot the rest of what Jesus said at the dinner table. And it was the rest of what Jesus said that was full of promise!

Even after news of the resurrection, Peter was so weak, having been run out of his own strength, he told the other disciples:

"I am finished. It's over for me. There is no place for me here anymore. I can no longer be a disciple. I've done the absolute worst thing a follower of Christ could ever do. I've denied Him before men. I'm going back to fishing."

How Do We Define The "Victorious Christian Life"?

There are many of God's people who are so overcome by the shame of having their own strength crushed by unconquerable circumstances, they have given up. What they thought was going to be the *"victorious Christian life,"* has turned into a series of seemingly unending disasters. I know. I am one of those people.

For nearly thirty years of ministry, I helped plant churches, I pastored leaders, and I taught others how to overcome, believe for their breakthrough, and get their miracle. Then such an avalanche of adverse circumstances fell upon my life that I came to believe my faith had utterly failed.

Everything that had seemed to work so well for me in the past just stopped working. Everything that had produced what I thought was such good fruit, was now producing bitter herbs, thorn bushes, and desert places.

What made it all worse was that we were part of a church that was experiencing a genuine *"Book of Acts"* kind of revival. Thousands of people were coming from all over the country to experience the *"take your breath away"* presence of God. Miracles were happening, lives were being transformed, and souls were being saved. Baptisms took several hours because of the numbers of people who were coming to Christ.

> We were "in revival."
> But I wasn't revived.
> I was drowning
> in despair.

We were *"in revival."* But I wasn't revived. I was drowning in despair. The last phrase you would have ever used to describe what I was experiencing during that time would have been the *"victorious Christian life."*

Pray More, Give More, Believe More-

The more I sought God, the more depression overtook me. The more prayer lines I got in, the emptier I felt. While others were seeing angels, I was seeing failure. While others testified of transformation, I saw only darkness and despair taking over my mind and emotions.

The more money I gave in the offering, the deeper in debt I went. The businesses I owned, that had seemed to be so *"blessed by God"* for so many years, were now in bankruptcy.

After enduring four years of an unstoppable decline, I gave up. I had already given up all ministry involvement, after nearly thirty years of ministry being my whole life. Now I gave up on even pretending. I didn't go to a church service for nearly a year.

The Pain and the Shame of Dying-

The pain of hearing another sermon about the faithfulness of God, the pain of seeing another person prayed for, and experience the presence of God, the pain of hearing another testimony of how God miraculously met someone's need; it just hurt too much. Instead of being revived, I went deeper into despair. Finally, I just quit. I know this sounds bad. I would never recommend it. I just didn't know what else to do.

> I know this sounds bad. I would never recommend it. I just didn't know what else to do.

The shame of it all became unbearable for me. Watching everything I built, now wither and die, was just too painful and embarrassing. The word of God, that was supposed to be milk and meat to me, now became a weapon that beat me day and night. All those verses I used to preach to others, now tormented me. They mocked me. Where was my *"mountain moving"* faith? Where was my *"peace that passes all understanding"*?

I used to work hard at scripture memorization. Why wasn't the Word *"working for me"* now? Instead, those same verses now came flooding back to haunt me. My heart would break as I remembered Psalms 42:4-5.

> *"These things I remember and I pour out my soul within me. For I used to go along with the throng and lead them in procession to the house of God...Why are you in despair, O my soul? And why have you become disturbed within me?"* (Psalms 42:4-5)

That was me. I used to lead the people of God into His holy presence. I used to teach others the way of the Lord. But without realizing it, I did so much of it in my own strength. And now, my strength was gone. I was finally being exhausted of all I thought was good within me. In His love for me, He was running me to empty.

For the first time in my life, suicide began to look like a viable option. My wife, Linda, became increasingly concerned, as she helplessly watched me devolve into a person she had

> **In His love for me, He was running me to empty and it was scary.**

never known. Out of her loving concern, she would call me at random times during the day just make sure I hadn't done something out of desperation; something just to end the pain.

Linda Never Gave Up-

I lost faith. I gave up hope. But Linda never did. She knew she couldn't fix this for me but she knew God wasn't finished. Somehow, she just knew that God was still working His good will for me. She never rebuked, she never accused. She didn't know when, where or how this would all end. She just quietly held on to hope. And she stayed with me.

She was determined to be there when God met me. She was determined to see the Lord finish the work He began in me. She knew that I had more to say and she was determined to be there to help me say it. For those who have read any of my other books, you know I owe it all, first to Jesus, and then to Linda.

Peter Didn't Remember, And Neither Did I-

Peter remembered that the Lord said he would be sifted like wheat and he would utterly fail. But Peter forgot the rest of what Jesus said, so he lost hope. Peter forgot that the Lord said he would make it through this dark night, that he would turn around, that he would gain a strength that was not his own, and he would become a source of Christ's strength for his brothers.

> My wife remembered what Jesus promised even though I forgot.

Somehow my wife remembered what Jesus said even though I forgot. Somehow she understood that I had to be sifted; that my own strength had to fail. And somehow, she remembered something that I had taught others; something that I had let slip. She remembered Philippians 1:6.

> *"And I am sure that God, who began the good work within you, will continue his work until it is finally finished on that day when Christ Jesus comes back again."* (Phil.1:6 NLT)

When people ask my wife how she endured those dark years, she can't explain it. When they ask her how she put up with my anger, fears, and frustrations, she doesn't have a snappy answer, a catchy phrase, or a tried and true formula for faith.

She knows people want an answer that they can hang on to in their own time of trial and she has deep compassion for them. However, she didn't have miracle words to fix it for me, and she knows that just words won't fix it for anyone else either.
Linda is not called to be a *"platform teacher."*

But I can tell you what she is. She's a believer! She is utterly convinced that the Lord is good and His faithfulness endures forever! She assures her heart that through every trial, God will turn all things for her good. But she didn't learn that just from a book...even my books. She learned it the same way Peter learned it- through suffering and seeing God's faithfulness come shining through *in due season.*

When Peter finally hit bottom, he bitterly remembered all his foolish promises. But sadly, he forgot the promises Jesus had given him. Fortunately, Peter had a good friend named John. Even though Peter didn't remember, John did. And he wrote it all down so we could benefit from it.

Even though Peter didn't remember the promise Jesus gave him, his good friend, John, did. And he wrote it all down so we could benefit from it.

Peter remembered Jesus saying, *"You will deny me three times."*

But it's what Jesus said next that would make all the difference for Peter...and for us!

Chapter Seven

Trusting The Trustworthy One

We serve a God who is infinite in His nature and inexhaustible in His characteristics. It certainly appears from scripture that we, as created beings, will spend eternity getting to know this Almighty One whose *"depths are unsearchable."*

In this life, our minds struggle for some way to know and understand the One whom our hearts adore. After Paul had been serving Christ for many years, he wrote from prison to the Christians in Philippi and said the craving of his heart was still *"that I may **know** Him."* (Phil. 3:10)

Clearly, Paul knew that there was far, far more to know about God than what our eyes, ears and minds can comprehend. But he also knew there was a day coming when we would no longer *"know in part."* (1 Cor. 13)

In our attempt to describe this One who was, who is and who is to come, we struggle with human terms that will somehow help us understand this indescribable God. So we use words like omnipotent, omniscient and omnipresent. By these words, we mean that God is all powerful, all knowing, and present everywhere, at all times.

These are concepts that are hard for our natural minds to wrap around. It's hard for us puny humans, who don't have a clue what is going to happen in the next five minutes, to grasp the reality that God lives above and beyond time; that the past, present and future are all laid out before Him and He *"looks down upon time."*

And yet, this is what all true believers base their hope on- Our God knows the end from the beginning. Nothing takes God by surprise. He never looks at any occurrence in the natural or supernatural realm and says, *"Wow, I never saw that coming!"* Our God knows everything and He is unhindered by time because He lives above and beyond it.

> **God lives above and beyond time. He "looks down" on time.**

In fact, He created time and rules over it.

When God revealed Himself to Daniel as the One who always was and always will be, Daniel's response was to declare;

> *"It is He who changes the times and the epochs; He removes kings and establishes kings; He gives wisdom to wise men and knowledge to men of understanding."*
>
> (Dan 2:21)

Because he understood his God lived above and beyond time, Daniel had complete confidence that God was working His will, even in the affairs of the pagan kingdom in which he lived. Men like Abraham, Joseph, Moses, and Nehemiah all had this same confidence, even though they were dealing with kings and kingdoms that did not acknowledge their God, Jehovah. They knew their God was sovereign over all, and though they could rarely see or understand what He was doing, they rested in the faith of God's ultimate control.

The Confidence of New Covenant Believers-

When the apostles gathered in Jerusalem to decide whether Gentiles could receive the free gift of being made righteous through faith in Christ's offering alone, James speaks for the group and says that God knew beforehand that all this would happen because;

> "Known unto God are all his works from the beginning of the world." (Acts 15:18 KJV)

Paul echoes the belief of all the fathers of faith when he declares;

> "And we know that God causes all things to work together for good to those who love God, to those who are called according to His purpose." (Rom 8:28)

Paul is not saying that all things are good. His letters are filled with warnings about evil and the affects that sin has on both the believer and the world. But he is saying that our confidence rests in being assured that the Almighty God MAKES all things work together for the eternal good of His people.

Paul is also not being fatalistic and saying that Jehovah is some kind of "Grand Puppet Master" who orders every event, regardless of human choice.

It is clear, beginning with the fall of a third of the angels and then throughout human history, that God gives free moral choice to His creation. But Paul is saying that because God knows all things ahead of time, He is working His overarching purpose through all human history; both individually and in the nations. He uses the choices He already knows people are going to make as the very elements to accomplish His will.

Keep On Reading Because This Important-

I know this can get a bit tedious and even confusing. It's sometimes hard to grasp because we are talking about the Almighty God. But this is very important. If we don't understand that God knows all things before the beginning of the time, then we will never be able to stand with unshakable confidence in the trials and tribulations we must go through. I go deeper into why and how we must put our faith the *"timelessness"* of God in my book, God's Brilliant Cure...*for fear, shame and condemnation.* (available at markdrake.org)

Worry-Free Living-

Jesus told us that our ability to live a worry-free life is directly connected to our faith that the Father, to whom we belong, is ultimately in control of all things.

> *"Are not two sparrows sold for a cent? And yet not one of them will fall to the ground apart from your Father. But the very hairs of your head are all numbered. **So do not fear; you are more valuable** than many sparrows."*
>
> (Matt 10:29-31)

Even in the activity of prayer, Jesus made it clear that for prayer to come out of faith rather than fear, we must be convinced that our Father already sees our future.

> *"So do not be like them (Gentiles, pagans); for your Father **knows** what you need **before** you ask Him."*   (Matt 6:8)

Just a few moments later he says:

"You of little faith! **Do not worry then,** *saying, 'What will we eat?' or 'What will we drink?' or 'What will we wear for clothing?' For the Gentiles eagerly seek all these things; for your heavenly* **Father knows** *that you need all these things."* (Matt 6:30-32)

For us to pray out of a place of rest and not worry, faith and not fear, we must get very clear on this truth- Our Father lives above and beyond time. He rules over time and space. And, since we don't know what's going to happen next, we need to listen to what He tells us in His Word about our future. He knows what He is talking about!

What if Peter would have just kept listening? Of course, then we wouldn't have this important story to teach us one of the most important truths in the Christian life. I say this with the utmost honor and appreciation for Peter's life and struggle-

> **Everyone is good for something...**
> **even if it's to just be a bad example so others can learn.**

The Holy Spirit has given us the details of what Peter went through so we can learn the same thing he learned, hopefully without as much pain and heartbreak. Though our circumstances will be different, though they will be uniquely designed for us, we will all go through the same process of death and resurrection.
But, our failures are not written down so everyone can read about them.

That's one of the reasons I write about my own journey. So others can learn and have hope without having to pay the high price that so often comes with personal experience.

It's often been said that *"experience is the best teacher."* I must disagree. Ideally, *the experiences of other people* should be the best teacher. If we will learn from them, we don't have to suffer in the same way.

> **The experience of other people is the best teacher. That way you can learn without the painfully high**

Oh, we will suffer adverse circumstances. We will go through the same process of being run out of our own strength. But we can go through it with a supernatural peace and assurance that it is all for our eternal good.

Looking backwards, we can see that Peter should have kept listening to Jesus. But Peter, like us, was too busy defending himself to hear the amazing promise Jesus was trying to give.

Introducing The New Covenant, The New Way-

By comparing the records given to us by Matthew, Mark, Luke, and John, we get a full picture of the conversation that went on around that table in the *"upper room"* on the night Jesus was betrayed. And this conversation is extremely important for our understanding of the New Covenant that was soon to come.

In fact, it is in this conversation that Jesus mentions the New Covenant...*for the first time*! We have no record that He ever refers to a new covenant during His three and a half years of teaching. He was living and ministering under the Old Covenant. Most of Jesus' words can only be understood with this perspective. Why? Because most of what Jesus taught is impossible for people to do without the power of God <u>empowering</u> them from the inside. Introducing the New Way!

Allow me to make what may sound like a very dangerous statement. Most of Jesus' teachings and parables have been seriously, though sincerely misunderstood. I suggest they were not designed primarily to teach people how to live. He taught these impossible standards to show people how impossible it was to actually live out the covenant of Moses by the strength of our human promises of loyalty. They could only be kept by divine power. Jesus' teachings were taught to prepare people for the New Way! A way of life only the Spirit can produce.

> "...we have been released from the law so that we serve in the new way of the Spirit." (Rom 7:6)

In fact, the impossibility of fully keeping the *true* Old Covenant was designed by God to run us out of our own human effort and teach us to depend completely upon Him to make us holy. This has always been the reason for the Law; to completely exhaust us so we will not trust in human effort.

The "Upper Room" Conversation-

Though all the gospel writers give us insight into the *"upper room"* conversation, John goes into the greatest detail. John's Gospel is divided into twenty one chapters. But he covers the birth, life, and ministry of Jesus in the first twelve chapters. By chapter thirteen, we are already in the upper room, the night He was arrested, beating, and, finally, crucified.

The gospel of John, chapters 13-14-15-16-17, all take place in the 3-4 hours in the *"upper room"* and on the short walk to the garden. It is in these chapters that we have the unfolding of the New Covenant which was about to come.

It is hard to overemphasize the importance of this conversation. It is in these chapters that Jesus explains about His leaving and coming back by the Spirit to live inside of each of them, and in us.

This shift from the Spirit being **with** them, to soon be **living in** them, is the great dividing moment of covenantal history. Understanding these words of Jesus is the key to understanding, and living in, the New Covenant; the New Way.

> "I will ask the Father, and He will give you another Helper, that He may be with you forever; the Spirit of truth...you know Him because He abides **with you** and **will be in you**. I will not leave you as orphans; <u>I will come to you</u>."
>
> (John 14:16-19)

You can read much more about this most important truth of Christ actually **living inside us** in my book, <u>God's Brilliant Plan...searching for the easy and light life Jesus offered.</u>
(available at markdrake.org)

The New Covenant Previewed In Peter

It was impossible for Peter to understand it that night, but the drama that was about to unfold in his life would be a grueling illustrated sermon of how the New Covenant was actually going to work. He was about to learn what it means for:

> "...a grain of wheat to fall to the ground and die, <u>so that</u> it might bear much fruit."   (John 12:24)

He was going to be completely run out of his own strength. Everything that Peter thought was good about his well-intended human effort would be fully exhausted. It would utterly fail. It would die. And in his complete exhaustion, in his *"death,"* Peter would discover the truth of the Father's unconditional love and the power of His transforming grace.

Once he was run completely out of his own strength, he would find the strength of Christ's life living within him. Once he utterly failed, then he would find the Spirit's strength to stand. Once he found that he was completely unable to keep his promise in his own strength, he would find that the promises of God could work powerfully within him.

We remember the deeply meaningful words Peter wrote many years later. This is what he learned from the most devastating experience of his life, and what he knows we have to learn, too.

> "After **you have suffered for a little while**, the God of all grace, who called you to His eternal glory in Christ, will Himself **perfect, confirm, strengthen** and **establish** you. To Him be dominion forever and ever. Amen."
>
> (1 Peter 5:10-11)

The Words Of A Broken, Victorious Man

These are not the words of a starry-eyed novice, but a painfully tested man. These are not the words of a man who had everything go the way he wanted, but a man who was taken down a road he didn't choose. These are not the words of a *"strong man,"* but a man who found, in the midst of his embarrassing weakness, the strength of God living in him by the Spirit.

These are not the words of a man who had some kind of *"super faith,"* but a man who learned God will make all things work together for his good; even in the midst of his deepest failure. These are the words of a man who learned why God had to run him out of his own strength, and how he became deeply grateful for it.

The heartbreak he surely felt about what Jesus said to him in front of his friends must have been devastating. But it wasn't over yet. Much more had to die. Peter had much further to fall.

But just like Jesus promised, he was headed for a fall right into the plan and purpose of God! He just didn't keep listening.

**This story wasn't over yet.
Peter had much farther to fall.
But he was going to fall
right into the plan of God!**

Chapter Eight

Let Not Your Heart Be Troubled...Peter

John's record of the *"upper room"* conversation is filled with
words that had to be deeply troubling to the disciples...
AND promises that would have been amazing...
IF they would have just kept listening.

*"I am going away...but I will not leave you as orphans...I
will come back by the Spirit and actually live inside of
you...the Helper will teach you all the things you'll need to
know...I go to prepare a place in the Father's heart for
you...you will bear much fruit because the life of the vine,
My own life, will flow through you".*   (John 14, 15, 16)

These were amazing promises.   Promises that would fulfill
everything the prophets had spoken about for generations. But
the only thing the disciples seemed to hear was the disturbing
news that Jesus was leaving and that they would all fail Him. And,
of course, Peter takes the lead and argues with Jesus.

We must understand that Peter didn't see this as just disagreeing
with Jesus. He saw this as the kind of *"faith promise"* that we all
would believe was the right thing to
say. But Jesus saw it for what it was;
the human strength that nullifies the
work of grace within us. So it had to
die.

> **Peter believed
> this kind of "faith
> promise" was the
> right thing to say.**

But well-intentioned human effort doesn't die easily. Self-effort never goes down without a fight. And it can't just be wounded. It has to die!

> **Self-effort can't just be wounded. It has to die!**

So Peter begins to defend himself in a struggle to keep self-effort alive.

> *"You are not going away...if You go, then I am going with You...You can't leave us...if you are leaving then I want to go with you, now!...They may all forsake you, but not me...I am ready to die with You, I promise!!"*

Jesus Begins To Prophesy To Peter-

Jesus, the Prophet of whom all other prophets were only a mere shadow, begins to prophesy to Peter. And in this prophecy, we find both the problem Peter was going to face, and the promise of what God was going to do inside of him.

> *"Simon Peter said to Him, 'Lord, where are You going?' Jesus answered, 'Where I go, you cannot follow Me now; <u>but you will follow later.</u>' Peter said to Him, 'Lord, why can I not follow You right now? I will lay down my life for You.' Jesus answered, 'Will you lay down your life for Me? Truly, truly, I say to you, a rooster will not crow until you deny Me three times'."* (John 13:36-38)

Of course, this was devastating to Peter. He has just been told he was going to do the very worst thing any disciple could do; deny his Lord. To make matters worse, Jesus made this *"accusation"* in front of Peter's friends. It had to be devastating and deeply embarrassing.

However, if he would have just kept listening, he would have heard something else; something that would have filled him with hope.

Do You See It?
Do You See The Promise Peter Missed?

Right in the middle of Jesus' prophetic statement is the promise Peter could have put his hope in. But he stopped listening.

> *"You will follow me later. Peter, you are going to make it. It's going to be rough. It's going to be devastating, but you are going to make it and you will be eternally better off because of it."*

Luke records even more good news for Peter, if he would have just kept listening instead of rushing to defend himself.

> *"Simon, Simon, behold, Satan has demanded permission to sift you like wheat; but I have prayed for you, that your faith may not fail; and you, when once you have turned again, strengthen your brothers."*   (Luke 22:31-32)

Listen to these amazing promises:

> *-I have prayed for you.*
> *-Your faith will not fail.*
> *-You will turn around after this.*
> *-You will be a great benefit to your*
> *brothers because of this.*

Peter was so blinded by the suggestion that his promises might fail in the time of testing, he missed all of this. The answers to everything his heart longed for are found in these promises. But, *"he kept on insisting."* He was so locked into defending himself

69

and trying to prove that he, and he alone, had the strength of commitment to do what the others couldn't do, he missed all of these amazing promises.

Humility Or Humiliation-

The path to the transforming power of New Covenant grace is found in humility. Only when we really understand that our strength gets in the way of God's strength within us, that our ability gets in the way of God's ability within us, and that our human promises get in the way of God's divinely powerful promises working within us. Only then can we freely humble ourselves, admit the truth about our weaknesses, and be filled with the power of His transforming grace.

As painful as it often times is, the pathway to this kind of humility frequently requires us to be humiliated by the failure of our own best effort. Only when human effort dies can resurrection life be realized; and the death of our well-intended human effort can be very humiliating. However, any who will learn by that humiliation will reap the eternal reward of the transforming grace of God through the New Covenant.

Because of God's great love for us, He will lead us into situations where our efforts will fail. They must fail. Our human strength must fail for us to experience the strength of God within us. Our strength and His are mutually exclusive. We must choose.

Our failures are almost always humiliating. God doesn't humiliate us; we inadvertently choose humiliation when we choose to defend ourselves instead of humbling ourselves.

> **He will lead us into situations where our efforts will fail. They must fail for us to experience His strength.**

We humble ourselves by acknowledging the truth about our human weaknesses. This is exactly the position Peter was in as Jesus told him what was about to happen to him.

For Peter to have had any other response than self-defense would have required real humility, and he just wasn't there; not yet. However, he would get there. We will get there, too!

Lord, What Should I Do?

This would have been a perfect time for Peter to use good old common sense. He has been with Jesus for over three years. For over three years he heard Jesus say things that always came true. For over three years he watched Jesus do things that people thought were crazy; but they always worked out exactly as Jesus intended.

> **Now would have been the perfect time for Peter to ask, "What do you think I should do next?"**

Now would have been the perfect time for Peter to say,

> "Lord, since you obviously know everything, I can trust what you are saying now to be the truth. So, instead of continuing to disagree with You and argue about what You are saying, I have a question. What do you think I should do next?"

But Peter was just not at that place of humility; not yet. Instead of choosing humility, he chose self-defense. He will get to a wonderful place of humility, but only after a terrible bout with humiliation. And years later, he will be able to write:

> "To sum up, all of you be harmonious, sympathetic, brotherly, kindhearted, and **humble in spirit**..."
>
> (1 Peter 3:8)

71

*"...and all of you, **clothe yourselves with humility** toward one another, for <u>God is opposed to the proud but He gives grace to the humble</u>. Therefore, **humble yourselves** under the mighty hand of God, that He may exalt you at the proper time..."* (1 Peter 5:5-6)

You Are Going To Make It Through... And Become Far Better Because Of It!

What if you and I were sitting at a table in a local coffee shop and I reached across the table, took your hand, and said-

> *"You are soon going to suffer in a devastating way. Everything you have trusted in up to now will be stripped away. Your circumstances are going to fall apart and no matter what you do, you cannot avoid what is coming.*
>
> *However, I am telling you now so you will be able to hold on and keep your faith. You are going to make it through this! And not only will you make it through, but you will be eternally better off because of this intense trial.*
>
> *In the past you, have trusted in your own strength, your own ability and you own understanding. Yet, when this is over, you will be filled with the strength of Christ's resurrection life. You will be able to stand in the absolute assurance that **all** things must work together for your good.*
>
> *By the way, you will become a great strength to many others who will learn to trust the Father in all their struggles because of the price you will pay through this suffering!"*

What if I ended with this-

> *"This is what the Lord says to you ahead of time so you will be ready to stand when it all falls apart!"*

What if I said this, not in some flashy, phony, super spiritual way, but as absolute, God-inspired truth?

A More Sure Word Of Prophecy-

I am not claiming to have this kind of prophetic insight for you. I am only using this as an example of what Jesus said to Peter. However, if you knew what I said to you was truly from God, and you listened intently to everything I said, how would you feel?

Wouldn't you be more likely to stand through whatever trial came next? Wouldn't you be more likely to hold up your *"shield of faith"* and be able to quench the fiery darts of fear, worry, and anxiety that the devil would surely throw at you?

Wouldn't you feel empowered to actually rest in your trial, knowing that the outcome of your faith will produce all your heart has ever truly wanted; to know Him and the power of His resurrected life flowing through you?

Though I do believe in the true gift of prophecy, we have been given a more sure word, by which all other words must be tested; the written Word of God. Years later, after seeing that everything Jesus said came to pass and experiencing the New Covenant life that His words produced, Peter writes these words.

> *"We have also a more sure word of prophecy; whereunto ye do well that ye take heed..."*   (2 Peter 1:19 KJV)

You and I have a *"more sure word"* because the Spirit moved Luke and John to record this conversation between Jesus and Peter. This conversation is filled with promises you and I can cling to in our time of testing as God runs us out of our strength...for our eternal good.

The example I used of you and me talking together may be a feeble example, but I believe it does accurately portray the reality of what happened around the dinner table on that last night between Jesus and Peter. What a difference it could have made if Peter would have just kept listening.

It took him down some rough roads, but Peter learned the value of heeding **all** the words Jesus spoke, the *more sure word of God*, instead of his own words of human promise and self-defense.

But, of course, we weren't there. We weren't able to listen to this conversation. Peter's problem is he stopped listening too soon.

Our challenge is to read. Our problem might be that we stop reading too soon.

Here's a thought.
What if we keep on reading?
What if we get the bigger picture?
What might we learn?

Chapter Nine

We Must Keep On Reading

Jesus' prophecy to Peter is recorded in all four gospels. For us to fully understand all that was said, we must read, and reread it all together. Our own spiritual and mental survival may depend on understanding the full story.. The Holy Spirit, through John, gives us an amazing insight that we must not miss.

John's account is recorded at the end of chapter 13. However, the conversation doesn't end there.

The Problem With Chapters And Verses-

I am deeply grateful for the price our forefathers paid to insure that we have God's written Word, the Bible. Many believers gave their lives as martyrs so we would be able to open our Bibles and read the word of God.

The *"books"* or letters that make up our Bible were not originally written in chapter/verse form. Through a process that spanned from the 13th to the 16th century, scholars divided the books, or letters, into chapters and verses. Most of these divisions are very helpful for study because they help to divide the words into sentences and thoughts. However, in some places they do us unintended harm.

Of course, the solution is to simply develop the habit of reading through the chapter breaks to make sure we get the full meaning of the original authors. In most places, the chapter divisions are a great help, but John 13-14 is one of several places where the chapter division makes a very important difference. It is only in reading through the chapter break that we can truly see how Jesus felt about Peter and the absolute confidence that He had in Peter's heart and the outcome of Peter's life.

> **Develop the habit of reading through the chapter breaks to get the full meaning of the original authors.**

Jesus Was Not Finished Talking To Peter-

John 13 ends with the seemingly devastating words-

> *"Before the rooster crows in the morning, you will deny three times that you even know Me."*

However, if we keep reading, we find that Jesus isn't finished. He continues talking to Peter through the chapter break. These are the very next words!

> *"Don't be troubled. You trust God, now trust in me. There are many rooms in my Father's home, and I am going to prepare a place for you. If this were not so, I would tell you plainly. When everything is ready, I will come and get you, so that you will always be with me where I am. And you know where I am going and how to get there."*
>
> (John 14:1-4 NLT)

Wow, this is amazing! After Jesus told Peter he was going to utterly fail, He then said-

"But don't be overly troubled about this, Peter. You are going to make it all the way through."

"What?!" I Completely Missed This-

"Don't be troubled!?" "Don't be tormented!?"
"Don't be completely crushed and give up!?"

How could I have missed this amazing promise from Jesus directly to Peter? And yet, I missed it for years because I just didn't keep reading. Combine Luke's account with John's account, and then just imagine what Jesus actually said to Peter-

> I missed it for years because I just didn't keep reading.

-Peter, I have given the devil permission to sift you like wheat. There is nothing you can do to change what is going to happen.

-Before tomorrow morning your strength and your human promises are going to utterly fail. They have to.

-You are going to curse and swear three times that you don't even know me.

-But I have already prayed you through this and your faith with not be completely destroyed, although it will certainly look like it has.

-When this is over, you will turn around. This will not be the end for you.

-You will be completely run out of your own strength but you will end up with a new strength that is not your own.

-And, you will be able to strengthen your brothers.

And now He keeps talking to Peter in John 14:1-

-Do not let your heart be overwhelmed by what I have just told you about yourself, (Peter).

-You believe in God, (Peter), now believe in Me and believe in what I am saying to you right now.

-In my Father's house (heart) are many places to dwell and I am going there to make a place for you, (Peter).

-If this were not true for you, (Peter), I would have plainly told you that it was not true for you.

-This is true for you, (Peter), and you will end up where I am going, back to the Father's heart.

-When everything is ready, I will return and get you, (Peter), so you will always be with Me, in the heart of the Father!

Remember, John said in the beginning of his gospel that Jesus, the only Begotten Son of God, came from the "*bosom of the Father.*" (John 1:18) Now, Jesus says He is returning to where He came from; the bosom, or the *heart of the Father*. Jesus just promised Peter that He was going to make a place for him there, in the *heart of the Father*!

This Changed My Life Forever!

When I saw that Jesus was still talking to Peter, that He was assuring Peter that this horrible trial would not destroy him but actually make him better, it forever changed the way I look at suffering and trials. I have never been the same.

I can honestly say that I have never again feared that I would somehow fail so badly that I would be utterly cast away from the lovingkindness of God. If I love Him, if my faith is in His sacrifice for me, I cannot be disqualified by temporary failures in the midst of trials or suffering. In fact, being run out of my own strength is the only way to experience His strength growing within me!

I cannot put into words the joy, the peace, the utter relief I experienced when I saw this simple, but life-changing truth. I have never looked at suffering the same way again. And I have been empowered to face my failures and the trying of my faith, in a radically new way.

Of course, Jesus was speaking to all his disciples, assuring them they would survive the trial that was quickly coming. But, when read in context, it's clear He never stopped speaking directly to Peter. Though the promise was to all His men, I realized that Jesus was prophesying to Peter that the very thing he thought would be his _end_ was actually going to lead him to his _beginning_; beginning to experience the reality of the true New Covenant.

Now I understand how Jesus has used my own embarrassing failures to run me out of my human strength so I could experience the thing Peter experienced. The reality of the

> **The very thing Peter thought would be his end, was actually going to lead him to his new beginning.**

true New Covenant; _Christ living His life and His strength in and through me, too!_

I Never Saw This Amazing Promise-

I have read this story hundreds of times, but never saw this. I have preached on this passage many times, but never saw this. I have read the opening words of John 14 at many funerals without ever realizing what Jesus was actually saying. And that He was still talking directly to Peter.

Certainly, He was sharing a divine principle for all the disciples. Certainly, He was speaking to all of us who have believed over the centuries. But He was actually still speaking directly to Peter.

For the first time, I could see the great love in Jesus' words as He spoke directly to Peter about the traumatic events that would happen in the next few terrible hours. For the first time, I saw that everything that happened to Peter resulted in the greatest discovery of his life.

Peter was about to discover what it meant to lose his life and find the life of the soon to be resurrected Christ coming to live in and through him. As a result, I began to see that all this **had to happen to Peter** so he could discover this amazing New Covenant life. There is just no other way to experience His life.

> Feel the great love in Jesus' words as He spoke directly to Peter about the traumatic events that would happen in the next few terrible hours.

Trials Designed Uniquely For Each Of Us-

The same thing must happen to us. God must run each of us out of our own strength, our own understanding, and our own self-defense. The circumstances will be different for each of us. They will be uniquely designed for each of us, out of the great love God has for each of us.

Like Peter, we will be tempted to believe we have utterly failed. Our adversary will push us to believe that we have been disqualified and that we no longer deserve to be numbered as one of His disciples.

But Peter's story is not over.
It has only just begun.

Chapter Ten

What Did Jesus Really Say?

By comparing how each Gospel writer recorded this event, we can go step by step and examine what Jesus actually said around the dinner table that night; especially the parts they missed.

(I strongly encourage you to stop, now, and read the complete story as recorded in these passages. It's an important principle for understanding Scripture- Compare All Similar Scripture.)

> **Matthew 26:19-35**
> **Mark 14:17-31**
> **Luke 22:13-34**
> **John 13-16**

Let me give you my condensed version. Imagine you are Peter.

-*Before this night is over you will all fall away from Me.*

-*You will all be filled with sorrow but soon you will be filled with joy.*

-*I must go away so the Spirit can come and live in you.*

-*I will not leave you as orphans; I will come back to you.*

-Where I am going, you cannot follow Me now, but you will follow Me later.

-Simon (Peter), Satan has asked permission to sift you like wheat.

-I have prayed for you, Peter, that your faith will not be blotted out.

-When you turn around, Peter, you will be able to strengthen your brothers.

-Before this night is over, Peter, you will deny three times that you even know Me.

-I am going back to My Father's heart and I will prepare a place in My Father's heart for you, Peter.

Jesus Knew They Could Not Understand-

After three and a half years of listening to Jesus say things that were hard to understand, and later finding out He was always right, one would think the disciples would have just trusted that He knew what He was talking about. However, Jesus knew they could not possibly understand what He was saying because they could not possibly understand how the New Covenant was going to work; not yet. So He reassured them.

> *"When the Spirit comes, He will teach you all things and He will <u>bring to your remembrance all the things I have spoken to you."</u>*   (John 14:26)

Because they could not possibly have understood what all this meant, the words Jesus spoke filled the disciples with despair.

But Jesus knew that these things had to happen. He knew their understanding had to fail. He knew their strength had to fail. He knew their ability had to fail. He also knew their best, most sincere human efforts had to fail.

Only in the complete and utter failure of their strength, their effort, and their understanding, could they receive the truth of the New Covenant.

> *His resurrected life coming to live in them and live through them by His Spirit.*

Years later, Paul summed up the revelation they all received after their complete and utter human failure, when he wrote:

> *"I have been crucified with Christ; and it is no longer I who live, but **Christ lives in me**; and the life which I now live in the flesh I live by faith in the Son of God, who loved me and gave Himself up for me."*   (Gal 2:20)

Peter, This Is A Good News/Bad News Situation-

All the disciples struggled to understand what Jesus was saying. But Peter was singled out for the toughest words of all. This is the guy who said;

> *"Yes, Lord, I can understand how these guys might fail you. But not me!"*   (Matt. 26:33)

Let's again examine the words Jesus speaks specifically to Peter:

1) The devil has asked permission to test you.

85

2) He is going to sift you like wheat.

3) Your promises will utterly fail.

4) I have already prayed you through this test.

5) Your faith will not be completely blotted out.

6) You will turn around.

7) You will then have a strength that is not your own.

"Peter, This Must Happen To You"

It's clear from the way Jesus worded this statement, *this test was going to happen*; it had to! He didn't indicate to Peter that there was another option. There was no *"if"* in this statement. He simply told him what *was going to happen* and there was *nothing he could do to avoid it*. No prayer, no sacrifice, no amount of faith would enable Peter to avoid this utter failure...for his own good!

He couldn't go around it, couldn't go under it, couldn't go over it; *he had to go through it!* He had to be utterly exhausted, completely run to empty by it!

It would be a long time before Peter would be able to say that it was the best thing that could have happened to him. It was this utter failure that finally enabled Peter to experience the New Covenant, the miracle of grace, the reality of Christ living in and through him.

> **He couldn't go around it, couldn't go under it, couldn't go over it; he had to go through it! He had to be completely run to empty by it!**

Jesus told him exactly what was going to happen in the next few hours. This would have been a great time for Peter to ask, *"Lord, since You know all things, what should I do?"* He was finally able to say this several days after the resurrection, but he was not ready that night; not yet. Peter was too busy being offended and defending himself. He was too busy denying that he would ever do such a thing; rejecting the idea that God would ever allow such a terrible thing to happen to him, and that Jesus knew him better than he knew himself.

> Peter couldn't ask the right question, yet. He was too busy being offended and defending himself.

Was This From God or From The Devil?

We can have endless debates over what's *"from God"* and what's *"from the devil."* But one thing is clear; God allows the devil to exist and to work in this fallen world. And when He is finished with him, God will cast him into the lake of fire, forever. (Rev. 20:10)

This question of whether a trial is *from God* or *from the devil* doesn't seem to be a debate the early apostles spent much time worrying about. In fact, Paul writes,

> *"For we wanted to come to you, I, Paul, more than once, and yet **Satan hindered us.**"*　　　　(1 Thess. 2:18)

However, after making the statement, *"Satan hindered us,"* Paul never refers to this again. His next words completely ignore the work of the devil to hinder, as he continues on in the next verse:

"For who is our hope or joy or crown of exultation? Is it not even you, in the presence of our Lord Jesus at His coming? For you are our glory and joy."   (1 Thess. 2:19)

This would seem to have been a perfect place to give a teaching on how to overcome the devil. Yet, Paul just accepts the fact that sometimes the devil is allowed to influence some circumstances to hinder us *(he never hinders God!)* and if God wanted it to happen differently, then He would have simply changed the circumstances. The Bible is filled with overwhelming evidence that when God wants to change the circumstances...He just does!

But the idea that it was important for Paul to understand **_why_** God allowed the devil to hinder him doesn't

> **The Bible is filled with overwhelming evidence that when God wants to change the circumstances...He just does!**

seem to matter at all. He just went about doing the task that was given to him, trusting that the Father knew how to arrange the circumstances according to His overarching purpose.

Time To Move To The Next Town-

This same idea of simple trust in the Sovereign Father seems to run throughout the book of Acts. Again and again, Paul's team goes into a city, people come to faith in Christ, a riot breaks out, Paul's team leaves, and they go on to the next town.

I need to say that again. They just leave! They leave these brand-new believers and seem to fully trust that the Father will care of them and grow them up in Christ.

I have to be honest and say that this really goes against the way I used to believe. Years ago, my "*charismatic-miracle-believing*" paradigm just couldn't have agreed with what appears to be giving up and giving in to failure. My former belief was you fight. You rebuke. You bind the devil. You get a team of prayer warriors to *"lay down prayer-cover-fire."* You curse the ruling spirits and break the hold of principalities and powers. You don't just give up and leave new believers! But Paul did. He just left.

I wasn't there. I didn't see all the variables. I'm certainly not wiser than Paul. I don't know what to do in every situation. Perhaps there is a time for some, or all, of that *"spiritual fighting."* Yet, Paul didn't do any of it; and he never felt that it was a defeat. He clearly understood a truth I have not always understood.

Another important truth about Paul simply leaving when riots broke out- he was never embarrassed about it. He never felt a need to explain or make excuses. He simply decided leaving was the wisest thing to do. Paul never felt that he lacked faith. He felt no need to demonstrate his faith by challenging every enemy and he didn't act as if his reputation as a *"man of faith and power"* was on the line.

There Is An Enemy To Stand Against-

Certainly, there were notable times when Paul rebuked people who were being used by the devil. He taught us

> **Paul was clearly not focused on the adversary and his activity.**

that there is an enemy to stand against and to not be ignorant of the devil's schemes. He taught his disciples how to stand against the lies of the enemy by founding their lives on truth. But he was clearly not focused on the adversary and his activity.

Paul believed that God always had a reason for what He did and did not do; for what He allowed and didn't allow, and what He prevented or empowered. Paul even had a very clear understanding of the years he spent in Nero's prison.

> *"And I want you to know, my dear brothers and sisters, that <u>everything that has happened to me</u> here has helped to spread the Good News. 13 For everyone here, including the whole palace guard, knows that I am in chains because of Christ. 14 And <u>because of my imprisonment</u>, most of the believers here have gained confidence and boldly speak God's message without fear."* (Phil 1:12-14 NLT)

Paul's focus was on Christ, and His victory; establishing people in the truth of what had been accomplished through the Cross. He taught people how to rest in the Sovereign Lord, focus on what Grace was doing in them, believing all things worked together for their good (Rom. 8:28) and learning to give thanks in all things (1 Thess. 5:18). He taught them to be strong, but to "*boast in their weakness*" so they could be "*strong in the power of His might*."

> *"So now I am glad to <u>boast about my weaknesses</u>, <u>**so that**</u> <u>the power of Christ can work through me.</u> 10 <u>That's why I</u> take pleasure in my weaknesses, and in the insults, hardships, persecutions, and troubles that I suffer for Christ. For when I am weak, then I am strong."*
> (2 Cor 12:9-10 NLT)

> *"Finally, my brethren, <u>be strong in the Lord</u> and in the <u>power of **His** might</u>."* (Eph 6:10 NKJV)

These are not the words of a coward! They are the words of a man who has learned that his strength came from allowing grace, the power of Christ's resurrected life, to work in and through Him. Paul was a man who had learned that the path to God's power within us is to understand that acknowledging our weakness allows His strength to be made real within us. He was also a man who didn't trust in formulas.

Paul's use of the words "*so that*" is critical to understand true grace. Just admitting I'm weak doesn't help unless it leads me to see that my honest humility makes it possible for true grace to unleash His power within me. I will admit my weakness **so that** His power can be released within me.

> "*I am glad to <u>boast about my weaknesses</u>, **so that** the power of Christ can work through me.*" (2 Cor 12:9 NLT)

It's important to note that there was no formula or method the apostles followed. They treated each situation as unique and trusted the Spirit to lead them in each case. They also learned to act as a team, as a body, rather than spiritual *"lone rangers."*

In this life, you and I will not be able to understand why or how the devil is allowed to do what he does. In the fullness of the Kingdom that is to come, we will

> **The early believers treated each situation as unique and trusted the Spirit to lead in each case. They did not teach formulas.**

understand it all, but not now. Our focus must be on learning to trust the Sovereign Lord and how He is leading us, in our weakness, to discover the secret of His strength.

I have come to suspect that much of my past "*warfare,*" from rebuking of the devil, to the effort I have put in making all kinds of *"faith declarations"* against the "*assignments of the enemy,*" were probably just wasted words. Sincere, but probably wasted.

Only after I was run completely out of my own strength, sifted like wheat, completely run to empty could I begin to understand what Peter learned through his devastating experience.

The circumstances that run us to empty aren't just to be endured, but each experience is filled with eternal truths to be learned.

Chapter Eleven

What Peter Learned Through Failure

Years later, Peter wrote about our adversary, the devil. His advice was to <u>stand firm in the grace of God</u> and <u>resist him in faith</u>. We resist him by standing firm in our faith; a faith that tells us that the Spirit is doing a good and necessary work within us. Somehow, beyond our understanding, God uses the devil in this process.

> *"Be of sober spirit, be on the alert. Your adversary, the devil, prowls around like a roaring lion, seeking someone to devour. But resist him, **firm in your faith**, knowing that the same experiences of **suffering** are being accomplished by your brethren who are in the world. After you have **suffered** for a little while, the God of all grace, who called you to His eternal glory in Christ, <u>will Himself perfect</u>, <u>confirm</u>, <u>strengthen</u> and <u>establish</u> you. To Him be dominion forever and ever. Amen."* (1 Peter 5:8-11)

"*Perfect, confirm, strengthen, and establish*" is what the transforming grace of God will do in us as we learn to *STAND FIRM in FAITH* while we endure suffering. This process is not for passive, faithless cowards, but believers who are learning to grow "*strong in the power of His might.*" (Eph. 1:19)

It requires genuine faith to trust that the enemy has only the power God allows Him to have.

It requires genuine faith to "*Stand Firm*" in the midst of suffering.

It requires genuine faith to believe that, in the midst of unrelenting trouble, the Father, Himself, will perfect, confirm, strengthen, and establish you.

Peter suffered deeply during the days after Jesus' arrest, beating, crucifixion, and resurrection. The fear, shame,

> **It requires genuine faith to "Stand Firm" in the midst of suffering.**

and condemnation he experienced because of his utter failure in the face of danger were the very things that prepared him to surrender completely to the work of the Spirit on the day of Pentecost. Peter tells us that this same work of suffering is being accomplished in us, and in all believers in Christ. We won't like it, but we can't avoid it!

When Am I Ready For His Strength?

After Peter had been completely run out of his own strength, he was ready to be filled with the strength of the Spirit. Only after his promises of commitment completely failed could he then receive the work Jesus had promised to do within him.

Remember, Jesus told him that after his failure he would turn around and be enabled to strengthen his brothers. This could only happen after his human strength failed, leaving him completely exhausted. It was a terrible process to endure. However, listen again to what Peter tells us about what he learned from this crushing experience:

> *"After you have **suffered** for a little while, the God of all grace...will Himself perfect, confirm, **strengthen**, and establish you."* (1 Peter 5:8-11)

94

When Peter wrote these words, years after his failure, he was strong. Yet, the strength he now had was not the strength of human commitment; it was not the strength of well-intended human promises. It was the strength of Christ living in and through him.

This strength only comes after we have been completely run out of our own strength. This can only happen after our human efforts have been completely exhausted. More often than not, this only happens when we suffer through trials, rather than be delivered out of them.

This can only happen when we are finally *"run to empty!"*

Peter, like me, fought this process every step of the way. He fought it because he could not understand it. He could not comprehend the process of death and resurrection; not yet.

Aren't I Supposed To Promise My Loyalty?

It was in complete sincerity that Peter *"kept on insisting...I will never betray you. I promise you, even if it costs my life, I will never fail you."*

This is the kind of promise that is highly valued in most Christian circles. Indeed, many of my most sincere sermons, passionate altar calls, and fiery youth camp messages have fervently encouraged

> Aren't We Supposed To Promise Our Loyalty?

people to make this kind of promise. Time, and time again, I have urged people to recommit, to rededicate, to recommit their recommitment, and promise to be faithful the next time; to *"put their hand to the plow"* and promise to never look back...again.

But is this really the way to build spiritual strength in the New Covenant? Is this really the way to grow the image of Christ within us?   Or are we just frustrating the work of true, transforming New Covenant grace by our human attempts to be strong? Could it be that we are actually getting in the way of grace? Or, as Paul put it- *"nullifying the grace of God"*? (Gal.2:21)

Here is the important lesson Peter learned through the suffering he endured during those days of fear, shame, and condemnation. These kinds of human promises only get in the way of the work of New Covenant grace.

> **Sincere, passionate human promises only get in the way of the work of New Covenant grace.**

Through this painful process of human failure, Peter learned that Jesus truly knew what He was talking about when He said:

> *"The truth is, a kernel of wheat must be planted in the soil.* ***Unless it dies, it will be alone*** *— a single seed.* ***But its*** ***death*** *will produce many new kernels — a plentiful harvest of new lives."*   (John 12:24-25 NLT)

Paul had to learn the same thing. (*We all must.*) He tells us that he has been crucified with Christ and that it is not he who lives, but Christ who lives in him. Then he tells us that he does not *"nullify the grace of God"* by trusting in the results of well-intended human effort. (Gal. 2:20-21)

Adverse Circumstances-

Here's my dilemma as one who believes in miracles. If I am not truly seeing all the Bible teaches about BOTH miraculous intervention and suffering, it can become too easy for me to reject the idea that God may allow adverse circumstances and not answer my prayer when, where or how I want. It can become too easy for me to discount the idea that He might allow temporarily bad things to happen to me for some higher purpose that I cannot possibly understand, yet.

However, the biblical evidence is overwhelming. Suffering through adverse circumstances is part of life in this fallen world, _SO THAT_, we can experience His resurrection life. And rather than get side-tracked into debates about whether God _"did it"_ or whether He _"allowed it,"_ I am learning that I am far better off if I just keep patiently watching, and see how He will work it all for my eternal good. That is His promise, after all. (Rom 8:28)

Understanding The Role of Adverse Circumstances Builds Faith-

Not only is suffering a part of this fallen world, but God uses all of it to accomplish the work of the Kingdom within us. Teaching us that when all else fails, our trust must be fully in His strength and not our own. This understanding is so very important that it was one of the first, foundational truths Paul taught young believers.

> After they had preached the gospel to that city and had made many disciples, they returned to Lystra and to Iconium and to Antioch, _strengthening the souls_ of the disciples, encouraging them to _continue in the faith_, and saying, **"Through many tribulations we must enter the kingdom of God."** (Acts 14:21-22)

Paul's teaching about the necessity of suffering through adverse circumstances did not make these new believers have less faith. It did not make them afraid or worried. On the contrary, the above passage says it _"strengthened their souls"_ because he was teaching them how _"to continue in the faith."_

97

> **Isn't this what we all want?**
>
> **To strengthen our souls
> and build our faith?**
>
> **Shouldn't we follow Paul's example?**

Keep Your Eyes On The Prize- Endurance-

After years of seeing the New Covenant working in the lives of every kind of believer, under all kinds of circumstances, the value of learning to endure trials which God chose to not deliver them from became clear. The early believers clearly prayed for miracles and experienced many. But they also understood the eternal value of endurance, with joy, when God didn't deliver them out of trials, but empowered them to go through them.

> *"Consider it pure joy, my brothers, whenever you face trials of many kinds, 3 because you know that the testing of your faith develops perseverance. 4 Perseverance must finish its work so that you may be mature and complete, not lacking anything."* (James 1:2-5)

> *"Blessed is the man who perseveres under trial..."* (James 1:12)

> *"We sent Timothy...to strengthen and encourage you in your faith, 3 so that no one would be unsettled by these trials. You know quite well that we were destined for them."* (1 Thess 3:2-4)

98

"Therefore, among God's churches we boast about your perseverance and faith in all the persecutions and trials you are enduring."   (2 Thess 1:4)

"In this you greatly rejoice, though now for a little while you may have had to suffer grief in all kinds of trials. 7 These have come so that your faith — of greater worth than gold, which perishes even though refined by fire — may be proved genuine and may result in praise, glory and honor when Jesus Christ is revealed."   (1 Peter 1:6-8)

Exhausted From His Own Strength, Run To Empty-

These hard lessons became an essential part of the foundation of faith in the lives of these new believers. These hard lessons came from understanding the painful experiences of men like Peter and Paul.

What Jesus told Peter that night, in front of his friends, was both painful and embarrassing.   However, Jesus knew that allowing the devil to sift Peter, to utterly exhaust him of all his

> **The only path to resurrection life is to be utterly exhausted of all our strength till our ability dies.**

strength, to press him until his ability died, was the only path to resurrection life.   Just as Jesus went through the combined suffering of all humanity before He could experience resurrection life for all mankind, so Peter had to be *"exhausted unto death"* of all his human effort so that he could experience resurrection life.

As painful as the Lord's words must have been, Peter's painful fall, his utter exhaustion and failure, had only just begun.

99

There was still more pain, more embarrassment, more room to fall, before he could experience the resurrection life of the New Covenant; the true, transforming grace of God!

**He couldn't understand it yet,
but Peter had a lot farther to fall!**

Chapter Twelve

How Can Failure Be Good?

Jesus has been arrested, beaten, put on trial, and crucified; it all happened just like He said it would. He has been taken down from the cross and buried in a rich man's tomb, just as it had been prophesied hundreds of years before. A large stone had been placed at the mouth of the tomb so no one could steal His body and later claim that He had risen, just as He had promised.

On the first day of the week, women came to mourn and anoint His body. When they arrived, He was already raised, He was alive; and they ran to tell His disciples. But the men just couldn't believe what the women said. They had all *"fallen away,"* just as Jesus said. Their own strength and understanding had been fully exhausted, for their own good, just as Jesus had prophesied.

Though this looked like utter defeat, and no doubt felt like complete devastation, it was actually the doorway into the greatest discovery these men were ever going to make. Far from being the failures they felt like, they were at the exact

> **Their own strength and understanding had been fully exhausted. Could it be for their own good, as Jesus had prophesied?**

right place, at the exact right time, for God to do exactly what He had purposed before the world began- *come and live in them*!

Was Jesus ashamed of them? Was He disappointed in them? Absolutely not!

How could He have been disappointed when He told them this was going to happen? How can He be ashamed of them when He told them that this, in fact, _had to happen?_

He knew that, rather than being failures, they were on the journey of discovering the true New Covenant. And the only way in was to be completely run out of their own strength so they could discover the strength of His life being lived in and through them.

> **Was Jesus ashamed of them?**
> **Was He disappointed in them?**
> **Certainly not!**

He knew the day would come very soon, when the broken, exhausted disciples would be able to say, as Joseph once said, _"The devil meant it for evil, but God meant it for our good!"_ So there was, indeed, great hope in their apparent failure!

There Is Great Hope Here-

All of this gives me great hope. It gives me hope because, even though they struggled with unbelief, even though He lovingly rebuked them for their _"hardness of heart and unbelief"_ (Mark 16:1-15) they were still His men. They were still His disciples, His people, His family. Their struggles did not disqualify them from being His men! In fact, it was these very struggles that prepared them to receive the true New Covenant and become His brothers.

And listen to how they struggled:

> _"Now after He had risen early on the first day of the week, He first appeared to Mary Magdalene, from whom He had_

cast out seven demons. She went and reported to those who had been with Him, while they were mourning and weeping. <u>When they heard that He was alive and had been seen by her, they refused to believe it</u>. After that, He appeared in a different form to two of them while they were walking along on their way to the country. They went away and reported it to the others, <u>but they did not believe them either</u>." (Mark 16:9-13)

"But these words appeared to them as <u>nonsense,</u> and <u>they would not believe them.</u>" (Luke 24:11)

Even when they saw Him alive, after the resurrection, they struggled with deeply rooted human fears and doubt.

"When they saw Him, they worshiped Him; <u>but some were doubtful.</u>" (Matt 28:17)

These were real men with real struggles. But they were struggling just like Jesus said they would.

> The only way they could experience the *New Way of life in the Spirit* was for the Old Way to completely fail; to be completely exhausted of their best human effort.

Their hope had always been in the Old Covenant which they thought depended on their knowledge, their understanding, their best effort.

But now they had to be run out of their *Old Way* thinking. Their focus and dependence on human effort had to change in order to receive the New Covenant. The *New Way* depended on their belief that God was the One doing the work within them and that He would finish what He started. And also, understanding that their human strength and understanding just got in the way.

103

The High Priest Of Our Hope-

In fact, their failure actually prepared them to receive the New Covenant that was about to come. Their failure was part of the dying process. There was no other way. They had to die to their own ability. They had to be run completely out of their own strength, run out of their own understanding, to be enabled to receive Him in His resurrected life. Everything was going to be different now. Everything had to change. What they used to believe, the way they used to do it, had to completely fail.

Of course, this was all beyond their ability to understand, yet. But Jesus did understand their dilemma and He knew this very painful experience was actually good for them. Remember, He is the *"High Priest who understands our weaknesses"* (Heb. 4:15). And rather than reject or disown them, He sent words filled with great hope to these frightened, guilt-ridden, doubt-filled men. *Because they were still His men!*

When the women came to the tomb they saw an angel who said to them these amazing words of hope:

> *"But go, tell His disciples <u>and Peter,</u> 'He is going ahead of you to Galilee; there you will see Him, <u>just as He told you.</u>'"*
> (Mark 16:7)

Does He Still Believe In Us?

"Tell My disciples."   In the midst of all this fear, failure and unbelief, you have to wonder what the disciples must have thought when they heard the message Jesus sent to them. *"You mean He still considers us as His disciples? After all, we are not even sure if we believe in Him. But apparently, He still believes in us!"*

What kind of hope would that pour into your heart? To know how much you have doubted, even considered it all *"nonsense,"* and yet, He still believes in you? Clearly, Jesus knew something about their hearts that didn't show in their actions.

> *"We are not even sure if we believe in Him. But apparently, He still believes in us!"*

Clearly, Jesus knew He was doing something inside of them that would take them through their own *"death"* and bring them into His resurrection life. They may have felt it was all over, but Jesus knew better. He knew the New Covenant was just beginning!

"Tell My Disciples, And Peter..."

Imagine what they all must have thought when they heard the words, *"And tell Peter to come, too."* They all knew what Peter did on that fateful night. You know the story must have spread like wildfire after all the promises Peter made at the dinner table just a few nights before. They all knew he had committed the one sin that must be worse than all the others; he cursed and denied the Lord. And yet, Jesus wants him included with the other disciples.

Why would Jesus have the angel say, *"...and Peter"*?
I can think of two possible reasons.

One might be that the other disciples no longer considered Peter to be part of the group because of his sin. But I don't think so. Considering how they all fell away, the unbelief they all struggled with, the unwillingness they all had to believe the testimony of all those who had already talked with the risen Lord, I think they all knew they were guilty of essentially the same sin.

My firm belief is that Peter had given up, counted himself out, and saw himself as permanently disqualified. He had already told the other guys, *"I blew it. I have utterly failed. I have been completely disqualified. I'm done. I just don't know how to do this new thing He wants from me. I'm going back to the only thing I know how to do. I'm going fishing."*

But then came the unexpected invitation.
"Be sure that Peter knows I want him to come to Me, too."

Wow, I would not have seen that coming. After all Peter did, after all his broken promises, I would not have expected for him to be invited to this post-resurrection gathering of Jesus' men. But clearly, Jesus saw Peter's failure much differently than I would have seen it.

> *"Be sure that Peter knows I want him to come to Me, too."*

I think we know how that invitation must have made Peter feel. He did come to Galilee, but he came with his head hanging down, ashamed of how badly he failed to keep his promises. But he did come. Overcome with fear, beaten down with shame, and fully expecting condemnation, he did come. Like Adam, hiding behind a bush in shame, Peter still *"drew near to God."*

The Answer Is Always The Same- Draw Near To God

Whatever you are struggling with, however you have failed to keep your well-intended promises to God, His invitation is still the same. *"Draw near to God and He will draw near to you."* (James 4:8) He is the Great Physician who always invites sick and broken people to come to Him for the medicine that will cure our brokenness.

Yet, somehow we have gotten this bizarre, destructive idea that we must first cleanse ourselves to show how serious we are. Then we can draw near to God. Much of this mistaken view comes from our misunderstanding of the Old Testament. Because we so easily misunderstand the judgments in the Old Testament, we have accepted a view of God's holiness as something of which we should be very afraid.

I was speaking with a young lady who had just finished reading the first five books of the Bible. I asked her if she could sum up the main message she got from what she had read. Knowing my own misunderstanding in the past, I was not surprised at her answer.

In all sincerity, she said, *"After reading about all the laws and the precise way they were told to build the Tabernacle, I would say that God must protect His holiness from unholy people."*

I completely understood her perspective. I had the same fearful perspective for years. But I don't believe that anymore. I now see that God has always been making ways for unholy people to come into His Holy Presence, safely, so they can be changed!

But this fearful perspective has been the lie our adversary has been using since the beginning of the human race. Adam and Eve hid from the only One who could cleanse them. The very reason we *"unclean creatures"* so desperately need to draw near to the most Holy God is because His holiness is medicinal.

Let me say that one more time-

God's Holiness Is Medicinal.
It can cure us!

God's holiness is what cures our unholiness. His holiness cleanses the carnality within us. Rather than fearing His holiness, we should love it for its transforming power. The Heavenly Doctor uses the power of His holy nature to change our unholy nature.

The reality is we can only see our need for His transforming power when our best human effort fails. It is only when circumstances run us completely out of our own strength that we learn to die and let resurrection life flow in and through us.

> **We can only see our need for His transforming power when our best human effort fails**.

Clearly, Jesus still had work to do to bring Peter to the place of inner truth. And it's only when we face the inner truth about ourselves that the New Covenant can do its work within us.

The only remedy for Peter's failure was to come when Jesus called.

Chapter Thirteen

Breakfast Gets Hard To Swallow

Luke tells us that Jesus appeared to the disciples numerous times during the forty days after His resurrection. He demonstrated with *"many convincing proofs"* (Acts 1:3) that He was indeed alive, just as He had promised He would be. In fact, everything was happening just as He had told them it would happen, including Peter's colossal failure.

John records that the third time Jesus appeared to them, He cooked breakfast on the shore while they were out fishing. It was at this breakfast that Jesus begins to talk directly to Peter.

When Must I Give An Account?

I can't imagine how Peter must have felt every time Jesus appeared. He had to wonder when Jesus would require him to give an account for what He had done. What kind of conflicting thoughts must have run through his mind? What a bizarre mixture of amazement, hope, suspense...and fear.

He knew it had to come up. Everybody knew what he had done. Everyone knew Peter would have to give an account for his actions. And Jesus finally brings it up. Or, at least, it sounds like He's going to bring it up. But it doesn't come out quite like I would have expected.

I can imagine Peter, and his friends, expected Jesus to at least ask him why he did it. Or, if he was sorry? Or, was he ready to repent? Or, tell him what punishment to expect.

Since the big argument around the dinner table that night was about who would be the greatest in the kingdom, surely Jesus would at least tell Peter he was demoted to the back of the line. Waiting for these painful questions must have made this breakfast one of the most uncomfortable meals ever.

> **Breakfast is hard to swallow when you're waiting for punishment to be handed out.**

But instead of demanding an explanation or issuing a punishment, Jesus begins by asking a strange question.

"Peter, do you love Me?"

And just like He did on the night of the last dinner, Jesus asks the question in front of the other men.

> *"Why does He keep bringing this up in front of the other guys?"*

Getting To The Truth About Our Well-intended Promises-

After all that happened over the last few days, what do you say to a question like that? After the most miserable failure one could imagine, how would you respond?

After all the arrogance Peter had displayed, all the accusations he made about his friends, all the self-defense he offered while completely ignoring Jesus' prophecy to him?

After all of his failed promises, what could he say to a question like this?

110

"Peter, do you love Me?"

At the dinner table on the night Jesus was betrayed, He was trying to get Peter to see the truth about himself and the truth about his ineffective human promises. Jesus was not trying to get Peter to crank up his will power, be strong in human strength, or make bigger and better promises. In fact, Jesus was trying to get Peter to do just the opposite.

But Peter didn't understand. He couldn't understand because it went against everything he had been taught about the Jewish Covenant. All his life, Peter was taught that a good Jew makes promises to obey God and he must keep them. But Jesus was trying to get Peter to see something entirely different. He was preparing Peter for the New Covenant.

To prepare him for the New Covenant, Jesus had to get Peter to see and admit the truth about himself and his inability. He was trying to get Peter to admit that he didn't have the human strength required, and then to see that his only hope was to listen and believe the truth that Jesus was telling him. Jesus wanted Peter to see, not just the truth about his human weakness, but to hear the promise Jesus was giving him about his future.

> **The only path to New Covenant life is to admit the truth about our inability to produce godliness.**

The Promise Jesus Made To Peter... And The Promise He Makes To Us!

"Peter, your strength is going to utterly fail. It must fail. But do not be overcome by this. Do not be utterly crushed by this. Your failure will actually turn out for your good because it will lead you to discover a strength that is not

111

your own.   This will be painful and embarrassing, but worth it! In fact, there is no other way."

Because we are looking back and see the end of the story, we know what Peter could not understand. Jesus was giving Peter a great promise about the true New Covenant that was soon to come. He was setting Peter up to experience the fulfillment of this great New Covenant. But for Peter to receive the true New Covenant, all his human effort must fail so Christ's resurrected life can come to live in and through him.

We know from this side of the cross that this New Covenant resurrection life can only come through the death of human effort. Jesus was trying to tell Peter that his best human effort actually got in the way of the New Covenant. And He tells us the same thing.

> *"Your strength must utterly fail. This will be painful, and embarrassing, but well worth it!"*

New Covenant life can only be produced by the death of our human effort and His resurrection life coming into us by His Spirit. New Covenant life cannot come through our human effort; it cannot be *"of ourselves"*.

> *"...and that, **not of ourselves**, so that no man may boast."*
> (Eph. 2:8-9)

> *"For what the Law could not do, **weak as it was through the flesh** (human effort), God did: sending His own Son..."*
> (Rom 8:3)

For us to truly experience New Covenant life, we must see the truth of the weakness of our human strength, the weakness of our human effort and the weakness of our feeble human

112

promises. Then, and only then, can we experience the mystery and miracle of Christ *living in and through us* by His Spirit.

> *"You are controlled by the Spirit if you have the Spirit of God **living in you**. (And remember that those who do not have the Spirit of Christ **living in them** are not Christians at all)...The Spirit of God, who raised Jesus from the dead, **lives in you**. And just as he raised Christ from the dead, **he will give life** to your mortal body by this same Spirit **living within you**."* (Rom 8:9-11 NLT)

Paul came to understand that human effort counteracted the transforming work of God's grace in the New Covenant.

> *"I have been **crucified with Christ**; and it is no longer I who live, but **Christ lives in me**; and the life which I now live in the flesh I live by faith in the Son of God, who loved me and gave Himself up for me. **I do not nullify the grace of God**, for if righteousness comes through the Law, then Christ died needlessly."* (Gal 2:20-21)

When Paul refers to nullifying the grace of God, he is telling us that if we try to make ourselves acceptable to God by human effort, we strip New Covenant grace of its transforming power. Our human effort to be *"good enough for God"* actually gets in the way of Christ's life at work within us.

The great promise of New Covenant life can only come through the death of human effort. Although that death is almost always painful and embarrassing, it is the very best thing for our eternal good. And, though he

> **His resurrection life can only come through the death of human effort.**

could not see it through his self-defense, Peter's failure was the very best thing that could happen for him. He couldn't see it yet, but his utter failure will bring him to the revelation of New Covenant life.

"Lord, You Know Everything"-

Trust is all about acknowledging that God knows everything and that we can depend on Him for the outcome of our lives. Jesus was trying to get Peter to the place where he would stop trying to defend himself and simply say, *"Lord, You know everything, so tell me what to do."*
Remember that during the last dinner, Jesus was trying to prepare Peter for the *"death"* he was going to have to go through. Jesus knew there was no other option for Peter. Peter could not change what was going to happen. He couldn't stop it, he couldn't go around it, and he couldn't avoid it.

All of Peter's human strength, all his human understanding, and all his human promises had to die in order for resurrection life to come. It was the only way to get to the New Covenant. And it remains the only way to experience New Covenant life!

Because we already know the outcome of Peter's struggle, we agreed in an earlier chapter that what Peter should have done was stop defending himself and say, *"Lord, You know everything, so tell me what I should do to get the best out of this trial."*

But instead of humbling himself, Peter fell into the trap of self-defense. He wanted to believe that he could change the outcome by making bigger and better promises to be faithful

> **We cannot change the outcome of suffering and trials by making bigger and better promises to God.**

114

and true. Peter kept insisting that he knew himself better than the Lord knew him.

Peter was trying hard to *"make a good confession."* He was trying hard to *"confess the word."* He was confessing promises of faithfulness from the Old Testament. He was confessing the things he believed a believer should confess. All Jesus wanted was for Peter to accept the truth about his weakness and inability, and keep listening.

The Lord really did know everything about Peter, but Peter was not ready to hear the truth about himself; not yet. So now, several days after Peter's failure happened, just as Jesus told him it would, the questions begin.

What Does *"Love"* Mean?

Now we come back to this seemingly strange question:
> *"Peter, do you love Me?"*

I spend much of my time in countries where I need translators because I don't speak the language. I have enough trouble with my native language, English, and about the only word I know in most other languages is the local word for *"bathroom."*

We English speakers do have a few challenges when it comes to certain words in the Bible because some Hebrew and Greek words don't translate well into English. *"Love"* is one of those words.

We can't understand Peter's struggle until we understand what he meant by "love."

The Greeks had several words to describe various kinds of love: God's love, brotherly love, romantic love, and etc. In English,

115

we just say *"love."* I say- I love Jesus, I love my wife, I love my children and I love to fly fish. But somehow, the word *"love"* doesn't truly communicate what you intuitively know I mean. My *"love"* for these different things is real, but it's not all the same. Clearly, I mean something different each time I use the word *"love."* Because of this, we can't really appreciate the struggle going on in Peter's heart and mind until we understand what he actually meant by the words he used.

Communicating Feelings Through Words-

When we read this conversation between Jesus and Peter in English, it goes basically like this:

> *"Peter, do you love Me?*
> *Yes, Lord, I love you.*
> *Peter do you love Me?*
> *Yes, Lord, I love you.*
> *Peter, do you love Me?*
> *Lord, You know all things, You know that I love You."*

When we read it this way we can't help but feel that something important is missing. It feels inadequate somehow. We feel like we ought to add more emphatic words like, *"Peter, do you **really** love Me?"* *"Peter, are you really serious this time?"* We feel this way for a very good reason; because Jesus and Peter are actually using two different words to describe two different kinds of love.

Agape And *Phileo-*
Two Different Kinds Of Love-

The two different Greek words used for *"love"* in this conversation between Jesus and Peter are *agape* and *phileo*. And the different meanings of these two kinds of love demonstrate how

116

uncomfortable this conversation must have been for Peter; and for his friends, as they listened in.

Agape is generally defined as God's divine love for us. It is also the word used to define His divine love living through us as Paul describes in 1 Corinthians 13. The origin of this kind of love is from God. The attributes of this amazing love will grow in our lives as we choose to put our faith in Christ living His life and His love through us by His Spirit.

As they sat around the table at that last dinner, Jesus told the disciples that this *agape*, this divine love, would be available to them after the resurrection. Why? Because this divine agape love would be accessible to them as the Spirit came to live in them through the New Covenant. But Peter and the rest of the disciples missed this awesome promise because they got caught up in the argument about Jesus *"going away."*

> *"A new commandment I give to you, that you **love (agape)** one another, even as I have **loved (agape)** you, that you also **love (agape)** one another. By this all men will know that you are My disciples, if you have **love (agape)** for one another."* (John 13:34-35)

This would have been a great time for one of them to say, *"Lord, this is awesome. Tell us how we will be able to love each other the way You love us."* But instead, Peter immediately says, *"Where are You going...You can't leave us...I am going with You...I will die with You"*. Jesus has to stop his arguing and self-defense with the embarrassing, but truthful words, *"Stop it, Peter. The truth is, you will deny Me three times before the rooster crows."*

The awesome opportunity to ask Him more about this amazing promise of agape love is lost because of self-defense and human promises. We always miss these great opportunities to learn more about God's everlasting love when we focus on our promises to God, instead of focusing on His promises to us.

The second word for *"love"* used in this conversation between Jesus and Peter, is the Greek word, *phileo*.

Phileo is generally defined as a human love, better described as *"brotherly love."* It is this Greek word from which we get the name, Philadelphia; the *city of brotherly love*. This kind of love is not bad, but it's inferior to agape because it's human in origin and depends on human effort.

The promise of the New Covenant is that the quality of our life and our love will be infinitely better than what human effort can produce. It will no longer be of human origin but divine, because Christ will live His divine nature through us. What an amazing promise of divine life and divine love. What amazing Good News!

But Peter couldn't hear any of this Good News because he was caught up in defending himself and insisting his promises were strong enough to stand. But now, days

> Peter couldn't hear the Good News if he kept defending himself.

after Peter's utter failure, Jesus brings him right back to face the truth about himself. Peter couldn't hear it at dinner, when he felt strong in his own strength. But he hears it now, at breakfast several painful days later, after his strength has been completely run out.

The Painful, Embarrassing Questions Begin-

Imagine we are standing on shore by the lake. The resurrected Christ appears to the disciples for probably the third time. So far,

118

nothing has been said about Peter's failure. And we listen in as Jesus begins to talk directly to Peter.

> *"After breakfast Jesus said to Simon Peter, 'Simon, son of John, do you love me more than these?*
>
> *'Yes, Lord,' Peter replied, 'you know I love you.'*
>
> *'Then feed my lambs,' Jesus told him.*
> *Jesus repeated the question: 'Simon son of John, do you love me?'*
>
> *'Yes, Lord,' Peter said, 'you know I love you.'*
>
> *'Then take care of my sheep,' Jesus said.*
>
> *Once more he asked him, 'Simon son of John, do you love me?'*
> *Peter was grieved that Jesus asked the question a third time. He said, 'Lord, you know everything. You know I love you.'*
>
> *Jesus said, 'Then feed my sheep. The truth is, when you were young, you were able to do as you liked and go wherever you wanted to. But when you are old, you will stretch out your hands, and others will direct you and take you where you don't want to go.'*
>
> *Jesus said this to let him know what kind of death he would die to glorify God.*
>
> *Then Jesus told him, 'Follow me.'"* (John 21:15-19 NLT)

Remember, this conversation happened because Peter failed to keep the well-intended human promises he thought he had the power to keep. Also remember, Peter did this because he thought it's what the Lord wanted him to do. He truly thought the Lord wanted Him to make these promises of loyalty.

Even now, it would seem to us that promising to be faithful to God is what a Christian ought to do. But Jesus was trying to bring Peter to the place where he could see the truth about himself, the truth about human weakness; not to hurt or embarrass him, but to help him come to the revelation of the New Covenant.

Aren't we supposed to promise our loyalty?

Chapter Fourteen

The Struggle With Human Love

Allow me to rewrite this conversation using the meaning of the Greek words *agape* and *phileo*, and how they were used by Jesus and Peter. Let's try to grasp what Peter was feeling.

This is so very important because Peter is finally seeing his weakness. He is no longer making promises. He is no longer ignoring the Lord's words. The humiliation of Peter's failure has brought him to a place of humility. He is no longer boasting in his strength. He is finally telling the truth.

"Peter, do you love Me with divine, agape love?"

"Lord, You know the truth; I love you as a brother (phileo)."

"Peter, do you love Me with divine, agape love?"

"Lord, You know the truth; I can only love you as a brother (phileo)."

"Then Jesus says, 'Peter, do you really love Me as a brother (phileo)?'"

Peter was grieved because He asked him the third time.

*"Lord, **You know everything about me**. You know that the best I can do in my own strength is love You like a brother (phileo)."*

"Lord, You Know Everything About Me"

Peter finally arrives at the place Jesus has been trying to get him to all along; the place of truth. He has finally come to the place where he sees that Jesus does indeed know everything about him. It's not pretty, it's not victorious, it's not filled with *"positive confessions"*; but it's the truth.

Peter finally sees that he is not able to produce anything divine by his human effort. He is now able to admit that even his love for Jesus is weak. Through his utter failure, Peter is at the place where he can admit the truth about himself and stop pretending he is stronger, better or wiser than he actually is.

But Jesus does not cast him away. He has not been rejected for his failure. He has not been punished. He has not been demoted. He is still counted as one of Jesus' disciples.

> Admitting the truth about our weakness prepares us for our own Pentecost

And he has finally come to the place Jesus has wanted him to come to all along. The place where he can say, *"Lord, You know everything about me and I can trust You to take care of me in my weakness."*

God Will Do What Is Needed To Bring Us To Truth-

It was this honesty, this truth, finally taking hold in Peter's heart, which saved him from his failure. If he would have blamed his failure on others, if he would have sought for an excuse, he would have never come into the New Covenant. His willingness to finally die to his own effort and admit the truth about his failure is the very thing that prepared him for what was to come at Pentecost.

King David had to come to the same place of truth. After years of running from Saul, hiding out like a hunted animal, God exalts David to the place that had been promised to him. But after being exalted, David's attitude about himself begins to change. The humility he had while enduring great suffering is replaced by the arrogance that often comes with *"success."*

As king, he now has a power he has never had before. He has the power to do what he wants. And what he wants is another man's wife.

> **Beware of the arrogance that often comes with "*success.*" Even *"success"* in prayer.**

After his sin with Bathsheba, and the killing of her husband, David is confronted with his sin. As king, David had the power to have the prophet who confronted him, killed. But David's response to the truth about his arrogant and willful sin was to confess the truth about himself. David's response was, *"I am the man."*

He didn't blame his wife for not loving him enough. He didn't blame her for not fulfilling his sexual needs. He didn't blame Bathsheba for tempting him by bathing where David could see her. He didn't blame God for not giving him the woman he wanted. He admitted the truth. *"I am the man."*

Most scholars believe David wrote Psalms 51 in direct response to the exposure of his sin.

> *"For I recognize my shameful deeds, they haunt me day and night. Against you, and you alone, have I sinned; I have done what is evil in your sight."* (Ps 51:3-4 NLT)

123

And then David comes to the same understanding Peter came to-

> "But you desire **honesty from the heart**, so you can teach me to be wise **in my innermost being**." (Ps 51:6 NLT)

God is always working to bring us to the place of truth about our weakness and the willingness to admit the truth about ourselves. God isn't interested in our defenses, our promises, or our declarations of faithfulness. He wants *"honesty from the heart."*

Trust In The Time Of Trouble-

Why does God place such high value on *honesty from the heart?* So He can teach us to trust Him *in our inner most being*. Only when I am brought to the place of truth and honesty can I learn how to fully trust Him. Trusting Him, trusting that He does, in fact, know everything, and that He will indeed work all things for our eternal good. Trust is what New Covenant life is all about.

But, as much as my flesh hates to admit it, the only time that trust truly matters is when things go wrong, when trouble comes, when suffering crushes me and God does not deliver me. Only when my strength is exhausted and I cannot figure things out by my own understanding; only then do I find out if I truly trust Him.

I Believe In Miracles...
And I Hunger For Honesty-

As much as I believe in miracles, as much as I know God does miraculously intervene in times of

> **The only time trust truly matters is when things go wrong; when trouble comes.**

trouble, I must learn to be truthful and honest. According to the

Scripture, He does not *always* intervene. And as much as my humanity hates to admit it, the Word of God is clear; suffering is an important part of the process of learning to trust Him.

Remember that Paul strengthened the faith of brand new believers in Acts 14:22 by teaching them that *"Through many tribulations we must enter the kingdom of God."* It is only through these tribulations that we learn to let go of human strength and understanding, and truly experience the power of the Kingdom of God alive within us. Just reading a good inspirational book won't do it...even my books.

These first century believers suffered in ways I cannot comprehend. But when I travel to some countries in the East I get a glimpse of believers who believe and see great miracles...and frequently suffer intensely for their faith without

> Paul strengthened the faith of brand new believers by teaching them about suffering, not by avoiding it.

deliverance. Many of them have an unshakable faith I dearly long for. But, I know that it only comes through suffering.

To tell people that if they just have enough faith, they will never have to suffer through troubles and trials is just not biblically honest and it's grossly misleading. To tell people that if they just have enough faith they will never get sick, or if they do, they will always get healed, and healed quickly, is just not scripturally true. And to tell people that if they just have enough faith they will never suffer loss, they will always prosper or they will never have to endure pain, is setting people up for crushing disappointment.

Each of these beliefs of guaranteed prosperity, health and success come from somewhere in the Bible. **But**, they come from partial verses, verses taken out of context or verses that don't tell the whole story until they are compared with other verses.

Peter was crushed by his failure because he didn't pay attention to all that Jesus said to him. When he failed, he only remembered a part of what Jesus said. Because he didn't remember all Jesus said to him, Peter's disappointment nearly killed him.

> *"Immediately, while he was still speaking, a rooster crowed. The Lord turned and looked at Peter. And **Peter remembered the word of the Lord**, how He had told him, 'Before a rooster crows today, you will deny Me three times.' And he went out and wept bitterly."*
>
> (Luke 22:60-62)

Half-truths Are Very Dangerous-

Peter remembered that Jesus told him his strength would fail and he would deny the Lord. But Peter only remembered part of what Jesus said. The *"half-truth"* Peter remembered was dangerous because it prevented him from trusting God's faithfulness for the successful "*end of his story.*"

> **Partial verses, verses taken out of context or verses that don't tell the whole story can very quickly turn into lies.**

Let's remember ALL that Jesus said to Peter.

> *"You will be sifted like wheat and you will deny Me. But I have prayed you through this crisis so your faith will not completely fail. And when this trial is over you will be able to strengthen your brothers."*

Remember what we learned about reading through the chapter breaks to understand context. So we keep reading because Jesus continued talking directly to Peter in John 14:1-3.

126

"Do not let your heart be completely crushed. You have believed in God. Now believe in Me and what I am telling you. There is a place in the Father's heart for you and I am going there to prepare that place for you so that where I am, you will also be."

When we read everything Jesus told Peter, we see that it was full of hope and promise. All Peter remembered was that Jesus said he was going to fail. This was true, but it was only a *"half-truth."* Instead of being strengthened by the Lord's promises, the condemnation this *"half-truth"* produced nearly destroyed Peter.

We face the same danger Peter faced. Half-truths can lead us to faulty beliefs that will crush us with condemnation. I know this danger because I have made the same terrible mistake and the condemnation nearly killed me.

So how do we avoid making the same mistake Peter made?

Is there a way to understand the process, embrace our inabilities, and rest in the dying process?

Could this "*rest from our own works*", trusting in the work only God can do; can this be the true Sabbath Jesus promised us?

Chapter Fifteen

The Embarrassment
Of Dying

I love to fly fish. It's my one real sports passion. I love Alaska. I love The Last Frontier, America's 49th state, for many reasons; the breathtaking landscapes, the amazing wildlife, the frontier mindset and the passionate believers. But the fact that it's one of the world's greatest fly fishing destinations certainly helps.

Catching a huge salmon, fresh and strong from the ocean, on a tiny fly rod, is great fun for me. But the life cycle of those beautiful, powerful

> **God uses the death of the old to bring life to the new.**

salmon is a dramatic illustration of how God uses the death of the old to bring life to the new.

Driven To Die

Salmon are born from eggs laid far up in the headwaters of tiny streams. Once the eggs hatch, the tiny salmon "fry" begin the dangerous trip down the river to the sea. Only a relative few survive this treacherous journey.

Once the tiny surviving fish reach the sea, they spend the next three to seven years, depending on the species, traveling the oceans in huge schools, feeding and growing. Then, suddenly, an uncontrollable urge clicks on in their brains.

They must begin the long journey of returning to the exact place where they were born. This urge to return is so strong they will do anything to finish their journey. They endure the long journey through the ocean until they find the mouth of the exact river they came down many years ago. Then, they begin to fight their way, against the relentless current, back up that original river. And they keep pushing their way up that ever narrowing river, no matter what the cost. They can't help it. The inner urge is irresistible.

After living most of their lives in salt water, once they enter the fresh water river, they begin to die. But they press on, exhausting all their strength, as their life drains out. They are driven by some incredible inner urge to return to the exact place they were born. Many of these huge fish push so hard that they end up in water so shallow; half their body is now out the water. Still they press on.

Once they arrive at the place where they were born many years before, females lay their eggs, males fertilize the eggs with sperm, and they die. These strong, majestic, beautiful fish just die.

Many die along the journey, becoming food and the means of life to other animals that eat them. Those who do make it to the end of this incredible journey, now become food for many other animals, birds, and insects. As their bodies decompose, they fill the water with life-giving nutrients for many other life forms, including the new fish that will soon hatch from the fertilized eggs; and the entire cycle begins again.

The Stench Of Death

By this time in the annual process, the strong and beautiful salmon have become a rotting mess. The smell is horrible as the decomposing bodies litter the banks of the rivers and streams.

It's an ugly sight. And yet, millions of living organisms, from thousands of giant brown bears to millions of microscopic insects, have been given life through the death of these majestic fish.

If it were possible for fish to experience human emotions, the embarrassment of this process would be horrible. Absolutely necessary, but terrible to experience. Shamefully embarrassing.

The Embarrassment of Dying To Human Effort

> **Peter's failure was deeply embarrassing. Death to self always is.**

Peter's failure, his death to human effort, was no less embarrassing. Some of our sins, the failures of our human efforts, are done in secret. But Peter's failure was done in front of everyone, written about by his closest friends for the future generations to read...and wonder about. And it was deeply embarrassing. Death to self always is. But it will always bring forth New Covenant life if we understand that God's process is always for our good.

> **The history of our "heroes of faith" is filled with the embarrassment of dying.**

The fear, shame, and condemnation Adam and Eve experienced when they sinned, came because of the failure of human effort. God wanted them to be completely dependent on Him for their understanding of right and wrong. But they ate the fruit hoping that they would gain the ability to discern right and wrong, good and evil, for themselves. If they could decide for themselves, they wouldn't have to constantly depend on God.

131

Remember, the tree was for the *"knowledge of good and evil."* The promise from the serpent was that if they ate, they would *"be like God, able to decide good and evil for your selves."*

Wait a minute. Isn't it good to want to be like God?

> Not when we attempt it apart from complete dependence on Him.

Isn't it good to want to be able to know the difference between right and wrong?

> Not when we attempt to do it apart from complete dependence on Him.

Jesus told the disciples at the last dinner, *"I am the vine and you are the branches. Abide in Me and you will produce much fruit. But apart from Me, you can do nothing."* (John 15:1-5)

New Covenant life is not about learning a list of *"Christian rules"* and then doing them by our own power. The branch cannot learn the rules about fruit production and then go off and do it by its own power.

> **The branch cannot learn the rules about fruit production and then go off and do it by its own power.**

The branch has no ability in itself, no matter how well it learns the *"rules."* It only has the ability to let the life of the vine flow in and through it. This is a life of complete dependence.

This is New Covenant life.

A Long History of Embarrassment

Hebrews 11 gives us a long list of *"heroes of faith."* It's a great history lesson of men and women who depended on God to do for them what He promised. But when we read their stories we find that nearly everyone went through deep bouts of embarrassment as they learned that human effort frustrated the work God wanted to do in them and for them.

Abraham was clear on God's promise to give him a son. But the waiting became too much. So Sarah and Abraham agreed together to help God out.

They came to believe the goal was to have a son. But God's goal was for them to learn how to trust Him. And the son they produced by their best effort became an embarrassment for the rest of their lives. In fact, the conflict between the son their effort produced, and the son God produced for them, still continues today.

They were clear on God's promise of a son. But they wouldn't trust Him for *when, where and how* the son would come. Their unwillingness to trust God for *when, where and how* His promise would be fulfilled caused them great embarrassment; but it didn't void the promise of God. Through their embarrassment, they learned how to wait for God to do what only He could do. They didn't start in faith, but they ended in faith. And the end is all that truly matters.

> **Trusting Him for the when, where and how is the true meaning of faith.**

Peter's embarrassment didn't void the promise Jesus made to him. On the day of Pentecost, Peter was empowered to stand up in front of the very people he was so afraid of just a few days before, and declare, *"Therefore let all the house of Israel know for certain that God has made Him both Lord and Christ; this Jesus whom you crucified."* (Acts 2:36)

The strength that Peter displayed on that day was not the strength of a well-intended human being making good on his promise. It was God's strength in a man who learned how to draw life and strength from the Vine.

And how did Peter learn this essential truth? Through the embarrassment of having his own strength completely exhausted and the painful death of his own best effort. Out of death came New Covenant life, completely dependent on Him, who is our life.

The Embarrassment Of A Mighty Deliverer

It was the will of God that Moses came to realize that, though he was raised as a grandson in Pharaoh's house; his real people were the Israelites. It was the will of God that Moses became grieved at how his people were being treated. It was the will of God that Moses began to feel that he should do something to free his people from their hardship.

But Moses gave into his feelings and acted in his own strength. His intention was good and God's intention was to use him to be the deliverer of Israel. But it was not God's time or God's way. It was the *when, where and how* that became the problem for Moses' faith. And because Moses misunderstood the *when, where* and *how* of God's will and timing, he fled Egypt afraid and embarrassed.

> **Moses failed because he didn't trust God for the when, where and how of God's will and God's timing.**

40 years later, God is ready to use Moses to deliver Israel. 40 years! That's a long, long time to most of us. And for Moses, the whole idea was unthinkable. He still felt the sting of embarrassment from his failed attempt 40 years earlier.

40 years ago, Moses wasn't willing to wait for *when, where and how* God would use him, and he utterly failed. But God's plan for Moses wasn't voided because of his failed attempt. In fact, Moses' failure 40 years earlier is what ran him out of any desire to act in his own strength. So he asked the important question, *"Who am I, that I should go?"* (Ex. 3:11)

We know that Moses wasn't unwilling to do the will of God, because after learning several important lessons, he did go. But he didn't want to act in his own wisdom, his own understanding, or his own strength. The embarrassment of his first failed attempt had done its job.

God's response to Moses is the one we must all look for. *"And He said, 'Certainly, **I will be with you**.'"* (Ex 3:12) 40 years before this conversation, Moses wasn't willing to wait for God to decide *when, where and how* He would implement His will. Moses now knows the *when*; *"I am sending you **now**."* (3:10)

Learning the *when, where and how* will be part of Moses' on-going education. But he did go in the strength of the Lord and we know the end of his story. Learning these things will bring many times of embarrassment, but the result will be worth it.

> Learning the *when, where and how,* and surviving the embarrassment, will be the largest part of our on-going education.

Joseph's Journey Into Complete Trust

Joseph is a great hero to all who walk by faith in God. And yet, we know of the many embarrassments he suffered. Some, because of his youthful arrogance, but most through no fault of his own.

We do not have the divine knowledge needed to understand why he had to go through all that he suffered. It also seems clear that Joseph never had full understanding of why everything happened the way it did.

But we do know this; the things Joseph suffered taught him to completely trust in God's care for him and to rest in His control over the events of his life. After years of suffering through the hateful, murderous actions of his brothers, Joseph was able to say, with absolute confidence:

> *"Now do not be grieved or angry with yourselves, because you sold me here, **for God sent me** before you to preserve life.*
>
> *"**God sent me** before you to preserve for you a remnant in the earth, and to keep you alive by a great deliverance.*
>
> *"Now, therefore, **it was not you who sent me here, but God.**"* (Gen 45:5-8)

Every time I read these words, I am nearly overcome. I stand amazed at the confidence and trust in God which Joseph displayed after all those years of *impossible-to-understand* circumstances. And to know that all he suffered was for the good of the very brothers who betrayed him! Amazing!

I don't pretend to understand all that happened to him. It's clear that Joseph didn't understand it all, either. He had to be willing to be run out of his own understanding, his own wisdom and his own strength.

Joseph had to become willing to endure the embarrassment of circumstances that certainly looked like God had utterly failed him. But his willingness to endure all of this formed him into a man of complete trust.

I want to be a man who is willing to endure circumstances that look like God has utterly failed me, **IF** it means I might be able to benefit others as Joseph did. Isn't that what you want, too?

But Joseph didn't start out this way. It took him years of very difficult circumstances to learn this valuable lesson. God gave him dreams and interpretations that helped people. Then God allowed those same people to betray him and forget him.

Years later, when his brothers finally came, he struggled intensely. He fought with a very understandable desire for revenge toward his brothers after many years of suffering. But he grew into a man who had complete confidence in the God whom he served. And his trust didn't depend on his ability to understand.

I want to be like him. I want, so much, to be a man who trusts like Joseph trusted. I crave to be a man who doesn't have to

> **It took Joseph years of very difficult circumstances to learn to trust God in things impossible to understand.**

understand my circumstances in order to trust my heavenly Father to work all things for my good.

If you are still reading this, then you must be a believer who is on this same journey. And after more than fifty years on my journey,

I have really good news for you. The Spirit of God is determined to do such a work in our hearts, that we will all be enabled to look at the adverse circumstances we face and know that the Father is working it all for our good.

He wants to empower us to be able to say with Joseph-

> "You meant evil against me, **but God meant it for good** in order to bring about this present result..." (Gen 50:20)

The Embarrassment Of A Pregnant Teenager

I doubt that any of us can understand the horrible embarrassment Mary endured as an unmarried pregnant teenager in first century Israel. We read the story of her giving birth to the Savoir of the world and we rejoice. But the truth of what she went through, what people thought of her, and what they must have said to her, and about her, is lost on us. We weren't there. We can't understand what she went through to do the will of God.

But, without disrespect, let's be honest for a moment, and put ourselves in the place of her friends and neighbors. *"An angel got you pregnant...with the Messiah?"*

By Jewish law, Mary could have been stoned. And Joseph took a great risk by stepping in and taking the blame for what happened to keep her from being punished.

"An angel got you pregnant...with the Messiah?"

They both willingly took on the shame of this apparent *"transgression"* for the rest of their lives. And, it seems that Joseph died without ever seeing the angel's promise fulfilled.

At least, Mary lived to see the resurrection, the day of Pentecost and multitudes come to believe in the Christ. Mary and Joseph had to be willing to die to their own understanding in order to do the will of God. And the shame of doing the will of God continued throughout their lives.

In John 8, Jesus is arguing with the Pharisees and at one point they say to Him, *"We are not born of fornication. We have but one father; God."* The insinuation is clear. They are attempting to mock Him because they knew the story of Mary's *"mystery"* pregnancy and the uncertainty of His parentage.

But it was this young teenage Jewish girl who believed what the angel said. She certainly didn't understand when, where or how. She certainly had to

> **The shame that came because of doing the will of God continued throughout Mary's life.**

trust in things she could not have comprehended with her mind. But she was willing to say to the angel,

> *"Let it be done to me, according to your word."*
> **(Luke 1:38)**

This is the kind of trust that all of God's people must grow into. And the only way to grow into this kind of trust is to be faced with circumstances that are impossible for us to understand. We can't understand them because we don't know the future.
But this is what we do know...

Our Story Is Not Over

Let's be honest. One reason we love the Bible stories is because they are over. We didn't have to live through them. They happened to other people and we get to read them. And we can skip to the end of each story and see, in retrospect, how it turned out so good. And they have become our heroes.

But if we would have been one of Noah's sons, helping build that huge boat, on dry ground, as they neighbors mocked us, it wouldn't have been such a great story...until it was over.

If we would have been part of David's men when the enemy came and killed our families, while we were following David to help out a neighboring king, it wouldn't have been such a great story...until it was over.

If we would have been one of Gideon's soldiers, greatly outnumbered, going into battle because our leader just heard an enemy warrior say he had a dream about a big *loaf of bread* rolling into camp and killing all our enemies, it would not have been such a great story...until it was over.

All of those people had to learn to trust. And that's what New Covenant life is all about; learning to trust that we are more valuable to the Father than any other creature and He will work all things together for our eternal good, no matter how bad things seem to be right now.

> New Covenant life is all about the faith to believe that He will do what He promised. He will come to live His life in and through us. All we have to do is believe He tells the truth.

My story is not over. Your story is not over. But our God will be faithful even when we struggle with our lack of understanding and our times of unfaithfulness, because He cannot change who He is- He is the Faithful God!

So we put our trust in the One who not only knows the future, but controls our future and He's weaving it all together for our eternal good! He has given us a faith-history that demonstrates His faithfulness in the lives of thousands of His people over thousands of years of trials and tribulations...for our good, always!

Though our stories are not yet over, we have His promise that He who started a very good and eternal work in us, He will finish it.

For I am confident of this very thing, that He who began a good work in you will perfect it until the day of Christ Jesus.
(Phil 1:6-7 NASU)

Chapter Sixteen

What Role Does The Devil Play?

What role does the devil play in the process of trials, tribulations, and the when, where, and how of seemingly unanswered prayer?

I don't know...exactly.
I don't believe any of us does know...exactly.
And, I am convinced we are not supposed to know...exactly.

Certainly, it's wise to understand our adversary to the degree we can. However, there is serious danger in going beyond what the Scripture teaches us about him and sliding into suspicion, speculation, and superstition. The devil would love for us to imagine him as being far more powerful than he is and make the mistake of reading far more into Scripture than there actually is.

Paul warned us to stay within the boundaries of simple and clear truth.

> *"Now, brothers, I have applied these things to myself and Apollos for your benefit, so that you may learn from us the meaning of the saying, "Do not go beyond what is written."*   (1 Cor 4:6)

Paul concludes by telling them that when we move beyond what the simplicity of Scripture tells us, we begin to *"puff ourselves up,"* by claiming we know more than others, or that we have *"special insight*." And when it comes to the devil, demons, and unseen spiritual powers, there seems to be a real temptation to "*Go beyond what is written*."

I do fully believe in the devil, the adversary, the accuser, the god of this world, prince of the power of the air. And, I also believe that these things all revolve around the war he wages in our minds, battling our beliefs, and twisting the truth.

As we read through the Scripture, it should become apparent, that we are not given enough information for us to fully understand the role of the devil. But, we must consider some of the clear truths we are told about the devil.

> **"Do not go beyond what is written."**

What We Are Told-

Without going into too much detail here, the Scripture gives us enough information to draw some important conclusions-

> -Lucifer was created by God to be a "ruling" angel; one of the three angels whose names we are given- Lucifer, Michael, and Gabriel. We are not given specific jobs for these angels beyond being servants of the most High God.
>
> -God gave him the free will to choose to continue serving the Almighty, but he chose to rebel, becoming the *"devil."*
>
> -It appears that one third of the angels chose to rebel along with Lucifer and these "fallen angels" serve with him.
>
> -Lucifer, now called the devil, is the tempter, the deceiver, "*the father of lies*."

144

-Jesus summarized the devil's activities, *"The thief's purpose is to steal and kill and destroy."* (John 10:10 NLT)

But remember, since we know that God holds the power of life and death, these words, *"steal, kill, and destroy,"* are metaphors. Important, full of meaning, but metaphors.

-Finally, we know God created hell to be the final abode for the devil and his angels. When He is finished using them, they will be forever banished. (Matt 25:41-42)

The Battlefield is in the Mind-

Most importantly, we are clearly told that the real battlefield is in our minds. We act the way we act because we think the way we think. His influence and torment is deliberately aimed at twisting truth so we believe lies about God.

> **We act the way we act because we think the way we think.**

With Adam and Eve, the lie was that God was withholding something important and good from them. With Abraham and Sarah, the lie was that God would not be faithful in giving them a son.

With the nation of Israel, it was the fear that even though God had miraculously delivered them from Egypt, He could not be trusted to provide food and water in the wilderness.

And with us, our enemy's attack is aimed at getting us to fear that God will not be faithful to us; that we are not valuable enough to God to be able to trust that He will do everything that's needed to take care of us. The lie is that we have to earn His love and care.

The accuser works to convince us that God's love and care for us is dependent on our holy, perfect behavior instead of God's great love for us, now, as we are, in our struggles. But, the truth is, *"We have a high priest who understands our weaknesses..."* (Heb 4:15)

Jesus' response to this fear is clear and definite; no room for doubt. In referring to how God takes care of all created things, He declares the truth-

"...you far more <u>valuable</u> to Him than they are..."
(Matt 6:26)

Peter learned, after his own meltdown, that God's loving care for us is what we can fully trust. He truly cares for us!

"Cast all your anxiety on Him because He <u>cares</u> for you."
(1 Peter 5:7)

Getting Clear About The Devil's Limited Power

We also know that the devil is clearly limited in his power, his knowledge, and his abilities. We must not give him more credit, influence, or dominion than he deserves.

<u>The story of Job gives us important insights to the devil's limitations.</u>

> *Then the Lord asked Satan, "Have you noticed my servant Job? <u>He is the finest man in all the earth</u>. He is blameless— a man of complete integrity. He fears God and stays away from evil." 9 Satan replied to the Lord, "Yes, but Job has good reason to fear God. 10 You have always put a wall of protection around him and his home and his property. You*

have made him prosper in everything he does. Look how rich he is! 11 But reach out and take away everything he has, and he will surely curse you to your face!" 12 "<u>All right, you may test him</u>," the Lord said to Satan.   "Do whatever you want with everything he possesses, but don't harm him physically." So Satan left the Lord's presence.   (Job 1:8-12 NLT)

God declared that Job was a truly upright and righteous man. In order to "*attack*" Job, the devil had to get permission and could only go as far as God allowed. Scholars, wiser than I, have written, "*The devil is an adversary on a leash who can only do what God allows.*"

Then the Lord asked Satan, "Have you noticed my servant Job? <u>He is the finest man in all the earth.</u> He is blameless— <u>a man of complete integrity.</u> He fears God and stays away from evil. And <u>he has maintained his integrity</u>, even though you urged me to harm him without cause." 4 Satan replied to the Lord, "Skin for skin! A man will give up everything he has to save his life. 5 But reach out and take away his health, and he will surely curse you to your face!" 6 "All right, do with him as you please," the Lord said to Satan. "But spare his life."   (Job 2:3-7 NLT)

Again, the Scripture clearly shows us that the devil had to get permission to torment Job and he could not go beyond what God allowed.

There are those in what might be called the "extreme word of faith" belief who say that Job brought all these terrible things upon himself because of his fears and negative words. But, the Scripture

> **As with Peter, the devil could not go beyond what God allowed.**

147

tells us that God considered Job to be blameless and upright in his integrity. Rather than "*going beyond what is written*," we must see what the rest of Scripture has to say about Job. If not, our suppositions may lead us into superstition.

The Lesson Learned From Job

We have come far enough in our searching of Scripture to know that every trial and tribulation is working in us the ability to persevere by faith while He works the very image of His Son within us. Although, we have no way of knowing exactly how trials and troubles all work together for our eternal good, we do know that the very things satan wants, which is to *kill, steal, and destroy*, are actually working just the opposite within us who belong to the Lord.

This is why John could say with absolute certainty-

> **"...the one who is in you is greater than the one who is in the world."** (1 John 4:4)

Although, God's purpose in giving us the story of Job has been debated for centuries, we do know how the first century apostles viewed Job's painful journey.

> "We give great honor to those who endure under suffering. For instance, you know about Job, *a man of great endurance*. You can see how the Lord was kind to him at the end, *for the Lord is full of tenderness and mercy*." (James 5:11 NLT)

Many first century believers saw amazing times of miraculous intervention. And, many of them endured times of extreme suffering without that miraculous intervention. Yet, they experienced an abundant life of *"righteous, peace, and joy in the Holy Spirit."* (Rom 14:17) For us to experience the kind of life the early believers experienced, we must view the work of the enemy in the same way they did. The early believers tell us the conclusion we must draw from all the terrible things Job endured is that "*the Lord is full of tenderness and mercy.*"

Job endured nearly unspeakable hardship but, because of God's compassion and mercy, this is what he learned through all the pain and confusion-

> *Job replied to the Lord: "I know that <u>You can do all things</u> and <u>no plan of yours can be thwarted</u>."*   (Job 42:1-2)

That's it! This the way I want to live my life! I want to live in complete confidence that no matter what trouble comes, no matter how I may *"be sifted,"* tested, and tried by the attacks of the devil, I want to base my trust on this eternal fact- *"Nothing can thwart Your plans for me, oh God!"*

This is not to minimize that, *"The thief comes only to steal, to kill, and destroy."* (John 10:10) But, it does show us that his efforts are limited to only what the Father allows. Why our Father allows seemingly "*bad*" things to happen

> *"I know that You can do all things and no plan of Yours can be thwarted."*

to us, his children, is far beyond our comprehension which is why it's always a matter of trust.

I know there are those who believe every "*bad thing*" comes from the devil and if we just have enough faith, we can live free of these "*bad*" trials and troubles. Or, if we just have enough faith, we can quickly overcome anything that stands in our way. I have heard sincere Bible teachers say, *"If human parents allowed an evil person to do bad things to their kids just so they would learn a lesson, they would be guilty of committing child abuse. And God is not a child abuser."*

However, this is very faulty human logic. And, to think we can interpret divine, eternal processes which only God can comprehend is very dangerous to our spiritual journey. Understanding the role of our enemy must come from the clear meaning of Scripture; not from speculation, supposition, or superstition, that makes him into something far more powerful than he actually is.

Here is a clear biblical principle which I know is true, but I am not able to fully understand it-

> *"Although He was a Son, He learned obedience from the things which He suffered."*   (Heb 5:8-9 NASU)

I cannot wrap my brain around how, why, or what the Son of God learned through suffering, yet the Bible clearly says it is true.

We know the eternal benefits that came through the suffering and death of Christ. We know the Father could have prevented it all if He chose. But the eternal purpose for Christ's suffering was far greater than the suffering itself. Knowing this, we must not fall prey to faulty human logic as we work to understand God's transforming process through our circumstances. There is just a whole lot we will not understand in this life. This is all about trust.

Some Things We Do Know About The Devil -

Revelation 12:10 calls him *"the accuser of our brethren who accused them before God day and night..."* The attack here is in

our minds, trying to steal our confidence with condemnation and shame. The accusations come continually, day and night.

2 Cor. 4:4 tells us that *"...the god of this world has blinded the minds of the unbelieving so that they might not see the light of the gospel..."* (NASU)

Again, the battle is in the human mind, twisting what people believe, and working to keep them from the truth. He tempts, he accuses, he condemns, he lies. He messes with our minds and tries to twist what we believe. But he cannot force us into evil. And, he cannot control the outcome of our circumstances.

After all the *"sifting,"* trials, and failures Peter experienced, he learned much about the enemy. This is his advice to us—

> *"Your enemy the devil prowls around like a roaring lion looking for someone to devour. 9 Resist him, standing firm in the faith, because you know that your brothers throughout the world are undergoing the same kind of sufferings."* (1 Peter 5:8-9)

Peter describes our adversary as a *"lion who prowls and roars."* But a lion who roars seeks to frighten, not to attack and eat. And, Peter's instruction was not to run or fight, but to resist and *"stand firm in faith."* Why? *"Because you know that your brothers throughout the world are undergoing the same kind of sufferings."* But the end is always worth it.

> **A lion who roars seeks to frighten, not to attack and eat.**

When Paul describes of the *"armor of God"* in Eph 6:10-18, each piece relates to specific things we must believe. Important things we must believe about what makes us righteous, what gives us peace, and what our salvation depends on. He ends by telling the believers to keep praying "*in the Spirit,*" because, as we have learned, the Spirit prays according to the "*perfect will of God.*"

He, also, tells us in verse 11 that the purpose for this metaphorical "*armor*" is not so we can fight the devil, but so we can stand in times of trial, unshakable, immovable...no matter what!

The battle is to believe the right things about-

-what Christ has done for us,
-what He is doing in us, right now,
-how deeply He loves and cares for us now,
-how we can keep standing, no matter what may come.

Beware of Complicated Teaching-

We must be careful that we don't get entangled in some of the teaching out there that seem to make our ability to stand and live in victory so very complicated. We must wary of any teaching that claims there are complicated things we must learn about the devil, demons, principalities, and powers. Just be careful.

We are clearly told that everything we read in the Old Testament, though real to them, must be seen as shadows and metaphors for us. And all these shadows have been fulfilled in Christ's victory!

> "*These are a <u>shadow of the things that were to come</u>; the reality, however, is found <u>in Christ</u>.*" (Col 2:17-18)

Please believe me when I say that I believe most of those who make their teaching so complicated, do so because they sincerely want to see people set free. But, I am concerned that nearly all of the complicated teaching about spiritual warfare, tearing down high places, names of demons, territorial ruling spirits, and etc.; virtually all these things come from a misapplication of Old Testament events. We must agree with the early apostles that these Old Testament events are shadows that are meant to lead us to the full and final victory of Christ.

> "He canceled the record of the charges against us and took it away by nailing it to the cross. In this way, _he disarmed the spiritual rulers and authorities. He shamed them publicly by his victory over them on the cross._"
>
> (Col 2:14-15 NLT)

We are very wise to require any teaching about "_spiritual warfare_" to be clearly confirmed in the New Testament epistles. The apostles based their beliefs about our relationship with spiritual powers firmly on the fact that Jesus' death and resurrection fully defeated them all. They simply believed in this victory and so should we. By His triumph over sin, death, and the grave, Jesus put every spiritual adversary to open shame!

The battle for us goes on in the minds of all of us. It is a real, but simple battle of believing simple truth. The truth that we are more valuable to Him than any created thing. The truth that He cares for us beyond anything we can yet comprehend.

> **We must simply believe the simple truth of His triumph.**

And, how important is it for us to believe in how much He _values_ and _cares_ for us?

It may well be the most important truth in our lives!

Chapter Seventeen

So Simple, Yet So Powerful

Believing that the Almighty God truly values you, right now?
Believing that He completely cares for you, for your very best?

Can it be so simple, and yet, so powerful? Yes, indeed!!

This brings us to perhaps our most important question, at least in regards to our trials, troubles, and prayer. The answer to this question will crush condemnation and fill us with supernatural peace. The answer will always bring the peace that defines all human explanation. The answer will keep renewing our minds, transforming us into people who are unshakable in times of trial.

And the question is this-

>   -What gives us frail, weak, extremely fallible human beings the opportunity, the right, to ask the infallible, Almighty God to help us?

>   -What right do we have to expect that the One who spoke and the universe leapt into existence; to expect that He will actually use this unlimited power to meet our needs?

>   -What gives us the right to ask Him for help...and fully expect that He will do it?

The answer to this basic question will settle all worries, all fears. The answer will wash away our doubts and fill us with confidence. The answer will renew our minds each time we meditate on it.

The answer is this-

> *We are more <u>valuable</u> to Him than any other created thing!*
>
> *He <u>cares</u> for us, eternally.*
> *He always has and always will.*

And because we are so very valuable to him, because He cares so deeply for us, now, in our weaknesses and struggles, we can come boldly to His throne of grace and find everything we need!

The accuser says our weaknesses disqualify us. But His word says-

> ***"This High Priest of ours understands our weaknesses."***

The accuser says we have no right to expect the Holy God to help us "*unholy failures.*" But His Word says-

> ***"There we will receive his mercy, and we will find grace to help us when we need it most."***

The accuser says we should cower in shame. But His Word says-

> ***"So let us come boldly to the throne of our gracious God."***

The accuser says we have no right to expect His help. But His Word says-

> ***"Let us hold firmly to what we believe."***

I memorized this passage years ago. Every time I struggle in the grip of troubles and trials, I bring this up and meditate on its truth. My mind is renewed, my emotions are washed with supernatural peace, and my faith is empowered again.

> "So then, since we have a great High Priest who has entered heaven, Jesus the Son of God, let us hold firmly to what we believe. 15 This High Priest of ours understands our weaknesses, for he faced all of the same testings we do, yet he did not sin. 16 So let us come boldly to the throne of our gracious God. There we will receive his mercy, and we will find grace to help us when we need it most." (Heb 4:14-16 NLT)

-Let us hold firmly to what we believe.

-This High Priest of ours understands our weaknesses.

-Let us come boldly to the throne of our gracious God.

-There we will receive his mercy.

-We will find grace to help us when we need it most.

Can it be so simple, and yet, so powerful? Yes, indeed!!

Chapter Eighteen

Good News About Bad Times

We've spent a long time talking about the devil, struggles, and trials. The temptation is to fear trials and work to avoid struggles. But the early apostles had a very different view. It's not that they somehow loved suffering, but, that they kept their focus on the eternal benefits. And, so should we.

Here's the really, really good news-

> "When troubles come your way, <u>consider it an opportunity for **great joy**</u>. 3 For you know that when your faith is tested, your endurance has a chance to grow. 4 So let it grow, for when your endurance is fully developed, <u>you will be perfect and complete, needing nothing</u>."
>
> (James 1:2-4 NLT)

Can you imagine that you can be *"complete, needing nothing"*? It's true. You can!

> "So be truly glad. ***There is wonderful joy ahead****, even though you have to endure many trials for a little while. 7 These trials will show that your faith is genuine. It is being tested as fire tests and purifies gold—though your faith is far more precious than mere gold. So when your faith remains strong through many trials, it will bring you much

*praise and glory and honor on the day when Jesus Christ is
revealed to the whole world."*   (1 Peter 1:6-7 NLT)

We've read about Job, Joseph, Peter, James, John, and Paul. They
all knew there was a devil. They all knew his influence on the
human heart and mind was evil and destructive. But, they also
knew he was, and is, a *"lion on a leash"* who can only do what he
is allowed to do by the Almighty.

They had no fear of him for themselves.
They were aware of his limited *"schemes"*
and they had no worry that he would
somehow win in their lives. They were
completely convinced that there is One who is in complete control
of the circumstances in their lives. And they knew *"the One"* was
not the devil. They knew their Father ruled over all!

> **There is wonderful joy ahead!**

> *"One God and Father of all, who is over all and through all
> and in all."*   (Eph 4:6)

They understood this was NOT a universal contest between a
"good God" and a *"bad god."* They knew this was NOT a cosmic
battle whose outcome was yet to be decided. They knew that the
battled had already been won, that when He said, *"It is finished,"*
our eternal place with God was settled, once and for all. The
ultimate battle was truly over.

Paul declared the truth that all our *"heroes of faith"* somehow
understood. Giving us the absolute assurance in what Jesus
accomplished through the cross and His resurrection, Paul says,

> *"In this way, he disarmed the spiritual rulers and
> authorities. He shamed them publicly by his victory over
> them on the cross."*   (Colossians 2:15 NLT)

160

Their whole life rested in the unshakable knowledge that there is only God, one Lord, One Almighty Ruler of all. They understood that though the devil's "attacks" could be

"You will be perfect and complete, needing nothing."

truly painful, they were only temporary and served an eternal purpose in God's perfect plan. And they belonged to Him, so the outcome of their eternal victory was guaranteed.

Trials Come So That...

When Paul referred to the sufferings he and other believers endured, he nearly always used the words "*so that...*"-

> "*so that* we would not trust in ourselves, but in God who raises the dead." (2 Cor 1:9 NASU)

> "*so that* you will be able to endure it." (1 Cor 10:13 NASU)

> "*so that* we will be able to comfort those who are in any affliction with the comfort with which we ourselves are comforted by God." (2 Cor 1:4 NASU)

> "*so that* no advantage would be taken of us by Satan, for we are not ignorant of his schemes." (2 Cor 2:11 NASU)

> "*so that* the surpassing greatness of the power will be of God and not from ourselves." (2 Cor 4:7 NASU)

> "*so that* the life of Jesus also may be manifested in our body..." (2 Cor 4:10 NASU)

> "*so that* the life of Jesus also may be manifested in our mortal flesh." (2 Cor 4:11 NASU)

161

*"**so that** they who live might no longer live for themselves, but for Him who died and rose again on their behalf."*
(2 Cor 5:15 NASU)

*"**so that** we might become the righteousness of God in Him."*
(2 Cor 5:21 NASU)

*"**so that** always having all sufficiency in everything, you may have an abundance for every good deed..."*
(2 Cor 9:8 NASU)

*"**so that** the power of Christ may dwell in me."*
(2 Cor 12:9-10 NASU)

> ## *"So that we would not trust in ourselves, but in God."*

Let Me Be Very Clear-

I believe in miracles.
I believe God answers prayer.
I believe in miraculous interventions.
I believe in the supernatural gifts of the Spirit.
I believe in asking God to meets our needs in whatever way possible.

For over 47 years, my wife and I have pastored churches, traveled around the world teaching the Word, prayed for the sick, ministered in gifts of the Spirit, sought deliverance for severely oppressed people, and believed God for our financial needs to be met.

We have, also, seen the broken hearts and confusion in those who didn't get their miracle, didn't get their healing, or didn't get their financial needs miraculously met.

It's easy and wonderful to rejoice with those who have just been set free from excruciating pain, liberated from tormenting oppression, or had their impending financial ruin averted by miraculous intervention. But, it is a much different experience to watch a sense of hopelessness and utter confusion flood over people because their hopes have been smashed and disappointment has crushed them, because they didn't get the answer they so desperately needed. And now, all that's left for them is to suffer through fear, shame, and condemnation. Often times, the fear, shame, and condemnation can be worse than the actual problem.

This is why we so desperately need to learn to read God's Word as it is simply written, for what the simple truth says, and not go beyond what it says.

The cry of our hearts is that we, as Bible-believing Christians, would become mature enough, honest enough to see the plain and simple truth. God does sometimes miraculously intervene. And God does sometimes uphold us as we persevere through times of testing. Becoming mature requires that we experience both situations and not lose our confidence that He does work all things together for good.

One of the most misused passages in the New Testament, a passage so often taken out of context by sincere charismatic believers is-

"I can do all things through Christ who strengthens me."
(Phil. 4:13)

163

This passage is often used to "*proof-text*" the misguided belief that God will only allow "*good*" things to happen if we just have enough faith. However, Paul had an entirely different truth to teach us. If we are ever going to come to a truly mature faith, we must see the bigger picture. Through Paul's story recorded by Luke in the book of Acts, and the information he gave us in his letters, Paul saw amazing miracles <u>AND</u> suffered severe trials. Paul experienced miraculous, inexplicable interventions AND had to sometimes "*gut it out*" and endure times of great suffering. Both of these things were real life experiences for <u>ALL</u> early believers. And, as we have seen, much of the Scripture was written to encourage believers to hold to their faith and never "cast away their confidence."

> "*So do not throw away this confident trust in the Lord. Remember the great reward it brings you! 36 <u>Patient endurance is what you need now</u>, so that you will continue to do God's will. Then you will receive all that he has promised.*" (Heb 10:35-36 NLT)

So, we come back to the clearest statement we have about how we are to view both times of blessing and times of great trial. But, this time let's read it in context to get the whole, mature truth. This is where Paul's teaching begins-

> "*I have learned to be content in whatever circumstances I am. 12 I know how to get along with humble means, and I also know how to live in prosperity; in any and every circumstance I have learned the secret of being filled and going hungry, both of having abundance and suffering need. 13 I can do all things through Him who strengthens me.*" (Phil 4:11-14 NASU)

164

It is the word of truth that sets us free; free from fear, free from disappointment, free from worry, free from doubt, and free from condemnation. So let's focus on the word of truth from the apostle who wrote more than two thirds of the New Testament-

-Phil 4:11-14 NASU-

> -*I have learned to be content in whatever circumstances I am.*
> -*I know how to get along with humble means,*
> -*I also know how to live in prosperity;*
> -*in any and every circumstance*
> -*I have learned the secret of being filled and going hungry,*
> -*both of having abundance and suffering need.*
> -*I can do all things through Him who strengthens me.*

As we read through what Paul wrote to encourage the believers in Philippi, mature faith is clearly defined as faith that is content and endures in-

- poverty and prosperity,
- good times and bad,
- being fed and going hungry,
- having more than I need and not having enough,
- times of miracles and times of trials,
- I have learned the secret of living through both extremes

And, he finishes with this triumphant declaration-

I can go through all of these things, good and bad, because Christ strengthens me to do it all...

...and these circumstances will never change what I believe about Him!

165

Chapter Eighteen

Tying Up
Loose Ends

I realize that no one can even come close to answering all the questions about why seemingly "*bad*" things happen to believers, why sincere prayers seem to go unanswered, and why, even though the Spirit that "*raised Christ from the dead*" dwells in our mortal bodies, we don't see more miraculous interventions.

But, since I've chosen to write about this subject, I must attempt to answer a few questions that you have every right to ask.

1) Aren't you teaching unbelief?

-With all my heart, I truly hope not! My intent is to help us all grow in a mature faith that our God will be faithful to answer all of our prayers. But, to be true to the Scripture, we must be secure in the mature confidence that the "*when, where, and how*" of His answer is up to Him. And, it's always for our good! This must be the basis of our mature faith, the foundation of our hope.

> What we want is a mature faith, unwavering faith because it's founded on the whole truth.

> "*For in this hope we were saved. But hope that is seen is no hope at all. Who hopes for what he already has? 25 But if*

we hope for what we do not yet have, we wait for it patiently." (Rom 8:24-25)

Paul left us with clear examples of what true and honest teaching about trials, suffering, and prayer will do in the heart of a believer.

> *"After they had preached the gospel to that city and had made many disciples, they returned to Lystra and to Iconium and to Antioch, 22 strengthening the souls of the disciples, encouraging them to continue in the faith, and saying, "Through many tribulations we must enter the kingdom of God."* (Acts 14:21-23 NASU)

Paul taught these new believers that God does answer prayer, but not always when, where and how we want, and it actually strengthened their souls and encouraged their faith. It did not teach them unbelief, but just the opposite- it grew them into a genuine mature faith that trusted Christ to be Lord of all, over all!

2) If we can't be sure of when, where, or how God will answer our prayers, then how should we pray? What should we ask for?

-We should ask for what we think would be the best. Then trust the Father to do what we would have asked for if we knew everything He knows.

Of course, God knows that we do not know the future. We can't possibly know what the best outcome is for every situation. And, we certainly don't know our future and the future of all the

> **Ask for what you think is best. Then trust the Father to do what you would have asked for if you knew everything He knows.**

other lives that will intertwine with ours. So how can we ever know exactly how to pray, or what to pray for? We can't. And, the Father knows that this is our weakness when we pray.

> "In the same way, the Spirit _helps us in our weakness_. _We do not know what we ought to pray for_, but the Spirit himself intercedes for us with groans that words cannot express. 27 And he who searches our hearts knows the mind of the Spirit, because the Spirit intercedes for the saints in accordance with God's will." (Rom. 8:26-27)

Paul says the solution for our inability to know exactly how we should pray is to let the Holy Spirit, who lives within us, pray _in us_, _through us_ and _for us_.

> **The Spirit, who lives within us, prays for us, in us, and through us.**

3) How can I know if I am praying for the right thing?

-The beauty of being "_Spirit-filled_" is that the Spirit knows the perfect will of the Father. So, we should spend more time allowing the Spirit to pray in us, for us, and through us. Why?

> "...because the Spirit intercedes for the saints in accordance with _God's will_." (Rom. 8:26-27)

-Ask for wisdom in the midst of trials. Peter's mistake was he kept defending himself when he should have asked for wisdom.
"What should I do next?" James knew this.

> "Dear brothers and sisters, when troubles come your way, consider it an opportunity for great joy..._If you need_

wisdom, ask our generous God, and he will give it to you. He will not rebuke you for asking." (James 1:2-6 NLT)

-This is what James said we must believe- *Our God is generous with His wisdom and He will not rebuke us for asking!*

4) What if I ask for the wrong thing?

-That's not really possible; not if we ask in humility and trust. We can be at complete peace about the outcome of our prayers because we have a guarantee of success. He knows the perfect answer before we even ask.

> "And when you pray, do not keep on babbling like pagans, for they think they will be heard because of their many words. 8 Do not be like them, for <u>your Father knows what you need before you ask him</u>." (Matt 6:7-8)

So we are told to ask the best way we know how, and then trust. Tell Him what you need and let Him fill you with supernatural peace. Ask the best way we know how, and then trust.

> "Do not be anxious about anything, but in everything, by prayer and petition, with thanksgiving, present your requests to God. And the peace of God, which transcends all understanding, will guard your hearts and your minds in Christ Jesus." (Phil 4:6-7)

The only way to experience the peace that transcends all understanding is to trust the Lord as He leads us into circumstances that are beyond our limited ability to understand.

> **Ask the best way we know how, and then rest in peace and trust.**

5) Since God has the power to do anything, why does He not use His power to fix all my problems?

-Because He's after something far, far more eternally important than our immediate comfort. He is using every circumstance, every trial, every tribulation to form the image of His Son within us. And because His purpose is eternal, it is far, far beyond our extremely limited ability to understand now.

So we fix our hope on His promise that the trials which bring death to our ability, to our natural understanding, are working

> His purpose is eternal and it is far beyond our extremely limited ability to understand now.

a transformation that will bring us eternal enjoyment beyond anything we are able to conceive...yet. What He has planned for our eternity is beyond human understanding.

Paul had a revelation of the Spirit that enabled him to see that the extreme hardships he endured where the very things that were working together for his eternal good. And the "*eternal good*" Paul set his eyes upon empowered him to endure the most difficult of circumstances. Some, God delivered him out of and some, he had to suffer through. But he knew it was all worth it.

> "*...just as it is written, 'Things which eye has not seen and ear has not heard, and which have not entered the heart of man, all that God has prepared for those who love him.' For to us God revealed them through the Spirit.*"
> (1 Cor 2:9-10 NASU)

> "*For our light and momentary troubles are achieving for us an eternal glory that far outweighs them all.*" (2 Cor 4:17)

171

"I consider that our present sufferings are <u>not worth</u> <u>comparing</u> with the glory that will be revealed in us."
(Rom 8:18)

6) Since we shouldn't try to figure out the when, where, and how God is going to answer our prayers, what should we focus on?

<u>We have been learning Paul's perspective, in Romans 8, that-</u>

> *-we don't know exactly how to pray, and that's okay,*
> *-the Spirit prays in us, for us, and through us, and*
> *-we can be assured that the Spirit prays according to the perfect will of God.*

<u>Knowing these truths gave Paul the assurance that all things worked together for his good and he was being transformed-</u>

> *"And we know that <u>God causes all things to work together</u> <u>for good</u> to those who love God, to those who are called according to His purpose. 29 For those whom He foreknew, <u>He also predestined to become conformed to the image of His Son</u>..."* (Rom 8:28-29 NASU)

<u>Paul's ability to endure came from "*keeping his eye on the prize*"-</u>

> *"Therefore we do not lose heart. Though outwardly we are wasting away, yet inwardly <u>we are being renewed </u>day by day. 17 For our light and momentary troubles are <u>achieving for us an eternal glory</u> that far outweighs them all. 18 <u>So we fix our eyes not on what is seen, but on what is unseen.</u> For what is seen is temporary, but what is unseen is eternal."* (2 Cor 4:16-18)

172

Paul encouraged believers to set their minds on things above, on things eternal. To fix their eyes on the process that was working the character, nature, and image of Christ within them. And he knew the way to build the faith to persevere in his disciples was to talk about hardship and teach them to see the purpose for it.

> *"We do not want you to be uninformed, brothers, about the hardships we suffered in the province of Asia. We were under great pressure, far beyond our ability to endure, so that we despaired even of life. 9 Indeed, in our hearts we felt the sentence of death. <u>But this happened that we might not rely on ourselves but on God, who raises the dead</u>."* (2 Cor 1:8-10)

7) God won't ever give more than I am able to bear, will He?

Actually, yes, He will. And, we should be very happy that He does. He will do it because of His love for us. He will do it because He knows the eternal transformation it is working within us.

The reason so many believers have the idea that *"God will not give us more than we are able to handle,"* is because of a misreading of this passage-

> *"No temptation has seized you except what is common to man. And God is faithful; he will not let you be tempted <u>beyond what you can bear</u>. But when you are tempted, he will also provide a way out so that you can stand up under it."* (1 Cor 10:13)

Paul speaks here, not about trials and suffering, but about being tempted to do evil. No, God will not allow us to be tempted so

173

strongly that we can't resist it. But, He will, each time we are tempted, give us the ability to say *"no,"* **IF** we rely on his grace. When we don't rely on Him, we will fall to sin. When we do, the answer is to confess and take the blame, give thanks that the eternal price has been paid, and ask for washing, renewing, and His strength. And learn to trust Him the next time.

But, this far into our journey about weakness and failure of human effort, we must see that trials, trouble, and suffering are *"for our good, always!"*

I truly hope, with all my heart I hope, that the Holy Spirit has been speaking to your heart. That He has been renewing your mind and filling you with a great confidence in His process of *transformation through trouble.* My greatest hope is that we all come to understand the truth in Paul's inspired words; the truth that he learned through times of extreme suffering. He suffered so we could learn these truths at a much lower price. Many great believers throughout the ages have endured unspeakable suffering so we could learn to not rely on ourselves.

Again, we learn from Paul-

> *"We think you ought to know, dear brothers and sisters, about the trouble we went through in the province of Asia. We were crushed and overwhelmed beyond our ability to endure, and we thought we would never live through it. 9 In fact, we expected to die. But as a result, we stopped relying on ourselves and learned to rely only on God..."*

(2 Cor 1:8-9 NLT)

May the Holy Spirit cause these inspired words to renew our minds and strengthen our hearts with the truth that sets us free!

-We think you ought to know, dear brothers and sisters.
-We were overwhelmed beyond our ability to endure.
-We thought we would never live through it.
-We expected to die.
-As a result, we stopped relying on ourselves.
-and learned to rely only on God.

Isn't this the result we all want to rule in our lives?
To stop relying on ourselves and learn to rely on God?

This is the journey of learning to be *"led by the Spirit"* and I'm glad to share the road with you!

Would you consider joining us as a Legacy Monthly Partner?

Mark and Linda Drake

WHAT WE DO:
We Invest Every Effort In
Leaving A Legacy of Leaders

Our Legacy Monthly Partners Enable Us To:

1. TEACH, TRAIN, AND MENTOR younger New Covenant leaders around the world to go farther and reach more!

2. GIVE AWAY THOUSANDS OF FREE materials and **FREE TRANSLATIONS** in Asia, Africa, Central, and South America.

3. PROVIDE A FREE NEW COVENANT LIBRARY equipping leaders, world-wide, to read with a New Covenant mind.

4. DISTRIBUTE FREE TEACHING MATERIALS by email, flash drives and memory sticks to "*underground churches*."

5. *Ask*Mark **ANSWERS** "*difficult*" questions for people around the world, making Bible study simple, not shallow.

Our only support comes from dedicated people like you.

What You Can Do:
Build Your Own Legacy of New Covenant Leaders

The best spiritual investment of your money is in young leaders who will keep multiplying long after we are gone.

1. JOIN US RIGHT NOW as a Legacy Monthly Partner!
Go to <u>markdrake.org</u> and click the "Join Us" button.

2. SIGN UP for Mark's free **SMALL BYTES OF GRACE** and **SUBSCRIBE** to our iTunes Podcast.

3. SHARE OUR POSTS on Facebook.com/markdrakeorg, Instagram.com/markdrakeorg, Twitter.com/markdrakeint

4. USE *Ask*MARK FOR QUESTIONS that seem to contradict or confuse, and get email answers that are simple, not shallow.

5. PARTNER WITH US RIGHT NOW- Go to markdrake.org and click the DONATE button.

Our 501c3 non-profit gets the highest rating from the county, state, and federal IRS for how we handle our finances. Every dollar you give goes directly into building the next generation of New Covenant leaders, missionaries, and church planters.

PO Box 515080 St. Louis, MO 63151 markdrake.org

How We Handle Our Legacy Partner's Money
Mark Drake International

One of the highest honors we can imagine is handling your hard-earned money, investing it where it will do the most good, and doing it with integrity.   - Mark & Linda Drake

-Everything you give goes directly into our mission.
-We live a modest lifestyle because it right for us.
-We travel at the lowest cost reasonable.
-We give away as much as possible.
-We don't hire fund-raising companies.
-We don't purchase donor lists for solicitation.
-We do not use manipulation to prey on people's compassion.
-We don't make unscriptural promises of quick riches if you give.
-MDI, Inc. is an IRS 501(c)3 non-profit, tax exempt organization.
-MDI has been given the highest charitable rating possible.
-MDI is accountable to a non-paid board of directors.

-Want to see what you will be a part of?
Go to markdrake.org.

A few of the many resources distributed around the world because of the generous giving of our legacy partners.

These materials can help you grow in grace!

True New Covenant Grace is the miracle and mystery of Christ, by His Spirit, living IN and THROUGH believers. The result is a life that allows the fruit of His Spirit to freely flow through us while we rest in His promise to give us an *"easy and light life"* in yoke with Him. (Matt.11:28)

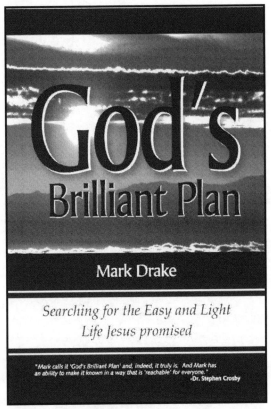

Many of the answers to how we can enjoy this kind of life can be found through the journey Mark has been on for nearly 50 years.

In <u>God's Brilliant Plan</u>, we see how God has been working since before the Garden of Eden to fulfill His desire to create a spiritual family that will rule and reign with Him forever. And, He is accomplishing this by putting His own spiritual DNA inside those who love him. This is the journey into true, New Covenant Grace.

The life-changing questions, *"What is God really like?"* and *"How does He really feel about me?"* are clearly answered here.

179

Mark's books are teaching and training believers around the world. The liberating truths in these books are being spread through hundreds of leaders into dozens of nations. God's Brilliant Cure...for fear, shame, and condemnation is a great follow-up to the truths learned in God's Brilliant Plan.

God's Brilliant Cure

...for fear, shame and condemnation!

"You can finally have confidence with God"

Mark Drake

Paul said, *"And we know, there is now no condemnation to those who are in Christ Jesus."* And, yet, it is clear that we don't really *KNOW* this because condemnation is the nearly universal battle for every believer, around the world. It doesn't have to be like this. He longs for us to live free, in righteousness, peace, and joy.

Fear, shame, and condemnation don't ever have to be a tormenting, harassing part of our lives.

Unshakable confidence should be our normal way of life in Christ!

When we truly understand the work Jesus did through His death and resurrection, and the transforming work the Holy Spirit that's being done within us right now, we begin to enjoy the life of freedom that is our birthright in Christ!

The question of whether women should be in church leadership has been debated vigorously for over 2000 years. Regardless of what you currently believe, the process of finding biblical truth is critical for all of us if our life is going to be *"founded on the rock."*

History shows that most first century believers were very uneducated and Mark demonstrates that God inspired Scripture to be written simple, clear, and easy to understand, if we read it correctly. Using 3 simple tools, Mark trains leaders around the world, in many languages, at all levels of education, to learn that the Scripture is actually Simple, though not Shallow!

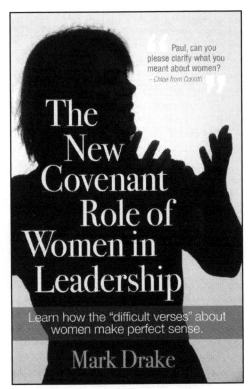

You can easily learn to use these 3 tools-
Consider Context, Comprehend Culture, Compare Common Scripture.

Have you ever wondered why-
-1st century women were almost never allowed an education, never allowed to testify in court, and considered equal to cattle?
-Why women were commanded to not braid their hair or wear jewelry?
-Why Paul sent the letter to the Rome churches by a woman?
-That the statements Paul made were only half of the conversation?
-That Paul never said for women to *"keep silent in the churches"*?
-Or, that Paul never said that *"women cannot teach men"*?

These *"difficult"* questions can be easily answered using these 3 tools-
Consider Context, Comprehend Culture, Compare Common Scripture.

Rock Solid Is Our New Covenant Discipleship Workbook.

Beginning with the miracle of the new birth,
-uncovering the mystery of how His Spirit lives in and through us,
-explaining the simplicity of reading and understanding the Bible,
-showing the importance of finding our place in the local church,
-handling our money with generosity and a growing trust in Him,
-ending with what we will be doing eternally in God's Kingdom,
Rock Solid covers how grace empowers every area of our life.

It's being used by believers, leaders, and churches around the world.
It's been translated into many languages and is given free to
missionaries, church planters, and pastors in a number of countries.
To find out how you may obtain free use of Rock Solid, go to
markdrake.org and click on "Translations."

MARK
DRAKE
INTERNATIONAL

WATCH

LISTEN

READ

JOIN US

Be Totally Transformed by the Mystery and Miracle of True New Covenant Grace.

Welcome to a wealth of materials to help you grow in Grace.

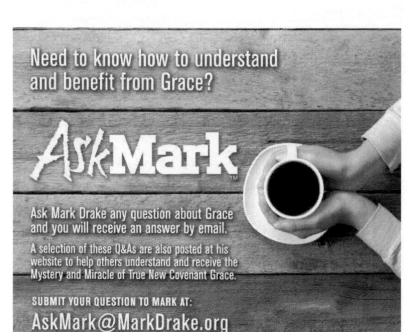

184

49940335R00107

Made in the USA
Columbia, SC
01 February 2019